5

STUDIES IN MODERN EUROPEAN LITERATURE
AND THOUGHT

General Editor:
ERICH HELLER
Professor of German
in the University College of Swansea

GERHART HAUPTMANN

Other titles are in preparation

GERHART
HAUPTMANN

BY

HUGH F. GARTEN

NEW HAVEN
YALE UNIVERSITY PRESS
1954

ACKNOWLEDGMENT

Acknowledgment is due to Messrs B. W. Huebsch, New York, for letting me use some of the translations from Gerhart Hauptmann *The Dramatic Works*, published by them. Apart from these, the translations are my own.

I also wish to express my gratitude to my wife for her help in preparing this book for publication.

H. F. G.

CONTENTS

Introduction

Among the major dramatists of the present century, Gerhart Hauptmann is probably the least known outside his own country. He figures in the histories of modern European writing as the author of some 'naturalistic' plays of the 1890's, several of which were produced abroad. But his later development, in fact the greater part of his dramatic and epic work, ranging over more than half a century, has remained almost unnoticed.

What explanation is there for this indifference at a time when Ibsen, Strindberg, Chekhov, Pirandello, O'Neill—not to mention the more recent French and American playwrights—have found full, if often belated, recognition? The first and most obvious reason is undoubtedly that a large number of Hauptmann's plays—and, for that matter, his most successful and most characteristic—are written in dialect, and that their essential flavour is lost in translation. However, there is a deeper cause which must be sought in the intrinsically 'German' quality of Hauptmann's work in general.

It is no mere accident that it was a dramatist who, during the sixty years of his creative life, was acclaimed as 'the greatest German writer'. For it can be said that in Germany the drama generally ranks foremost among the literary forms. A predilection for tragedy, for the sharp clash of passions, is deeply engrained in the German character. This is borne out by the role the drama has played in German literature for the last two hundred years. From the outset, the theatre has been regarded not so much as a place of entertainment as, in Schiller's phrase, a 'moral institution'. It is the platform on which the main issues of the time, social, moral, and spiritual, are joined. The drama is endowed with the full dignity of *Dichtung*; the dramatist is the *Dichter* par excellence: it is his essential task to create a self-contained world of independent characters who, wholly detached from their creator, enter into a life of their own.

Gerhart Hauptmann conforms fully to that ideal. His outstanding faculty is this very power of creation, of bringing to life a host of characters, each with his destiny, his individual soul. There is no rationally definable theory, no philosophy, no *Weltanschauung* which can be distilled from his work as a whole. What he has produced is a reflexion of nature, as multiform and contradictory as herself—but animated by a live and sensitive heart. 'A drama must move by itself, and not be moved by the author', runs one of Hauptmann's epigrams; 'the origin of its movement, like the origin of life, must be hidden to all'.

9

Gerhart Hauptmann had the rare fortune to win fame with his first play, and rarer still, to maintain that fame throughout a life-time. His was that true popularity which embraces both the intelligentsia and the mass of the people. This position he held all but unchallenged in the face of shifting literary fashions and rising generations, during a period of violent upheaval and revolutionary change in his country's history. The year of his birth, 1862, saw Bismarck appointed Prime Minister of Prussia. The earliest recollections of his childhood in the small spa of Salzbrunn in Silesia, where his father owned a hotel, are connected with the Austro-Prussian War of 1866. His adolescent years were spent in the newly founded Empire, with its shining façade of military might and ever growing wealth. After a few years at the *Realschule* in Breslau (years marked by material hardship, owing to the decline of his father's business) he was sent as an agricultural apprentice to an uncle's farm in the Silesian country-side. He did not prove a success. His creative urge first found vent in sculpture; for two years he visited the Art School in Breslau. At the age of nineteen he became engaged to Marie Thienemann, one of three wealthy sisters. Her parental estate in the Elbe valley near Dresden, with its romantic manor-park, formed the background for a phase of unclouded happiness. Under the guidance of his elder brother Karl, Hauptmann went to the University of Jena to read history and philosophy. A voyage through the Mediterranean, which ended in a prolonged stay in Rome, inspired a sprawling epic poem in the Byronic manner, *Promethidenlos*. From then onwards, the urge for literary expression got the better of his ambitions as a sculptor. At the age of twenty-three he married and settled down in Erkner, a quiet lake-side village on the fringe of Berlin, which was to be his home for several vital years to come. It was there that he wrote *Vor Sonnenaufgang*. The first performance of this play at the *Freie Bühne* in Berlin, in 1889, won him instantaneous fame. It was followed in quick succession by the nine or ten plays which made him, during the next decade, the undisputed leader of modern German drama.

The turn of the century marked, in more than one respect, a turning-point in Hauptmann's life. 'I feel as though I had reached the crest of a mountain range on which I am now walking', he noted in his diary. After an unbroken chain of successes, he experienced his first failures. In his private life, too, a prolonged and painful crisis, which left its mark on several of his works, ended in his divorce; and he married Margarete Marschalk, a young violinist, who remained with him to the end.

10

In Agnetendorf, in the foothills of the Riesengebirge, he built his house, 'Der Wiesenstein', which became his lifelong home, although as it happened he spent only a few months of every year there, dividing the rest, in an almost regular pattern, between the Italian Riviera in winter, the Baltic island of Hiddensee in summer, and the southern fringe of the Alps in the spring and autumn.

From the social critic and revolutionary whose plays were rejected by the censor, Hauptmann gradually grew into a national figure-head. Only once, in 1913, did he again come into conflict with the ruling powers of imperial Germany, when his Festival Play, commemorating the centenary of the War of Liberation, was withdrawn from the stage on account of its 'pacifist tendencies'. It was in the Weimar Republic following the First World War that Hauptmann's reputation reached its zenith. Although the time of his undisputed lead in the field of drama had passed, he commanded, by the sheer force of his personality and accomplished work, a universal respect unattained by any other writer. He was regarded as the embodiment of the noblest qualities of a nation purged of the pomp and bombast of imperial rule. In view of the whole-hearted support Hauptmann in his turn gave to the Weimar Republic, it seemed inconsistent that he should remain in Germany under the Nazi régime and, to all appearances, make his peace with the new masters. There can be no doubt that his reputation in the outside world would have been greater had he taken the course of so many other writers, and left the country. Without attempting to justify his decision, it is difficult to think of Hauptmann as an *émigré*. His entire nature was deeply rooted in the German soil from which he drew his creative powers; a transplantation would have meant mental stagnation. 'Nothing and nobody', he said at the time, 'can rob me of my right to the German soil'. Nevertheless, he was deeply aware of the changed world in which he was fated to live. 'My epoch', he said clearsightedly, 'ends with the Reichstag fire'. What he really thought, and how he suffered, gradually emerged after the war from the testimonies of his friends. His creative work during the last decade of his life shows no direct trace of the events that took shape around him—save, perhaps, an ever deepening pessimism and weariness which suffuse his final writings.

When the fighting line drew nearer to Germany's frontiers he left his home in the Silesian mountains for Dresden. There, in February 1945, he was forced to witness the destruction of the city which had been especially dear to him since his early

11

days. With his health gravely shaken, he returned to the 'Wiesenstein' where he lived for another year in what had become Polish territory. While the German inhabitants of Silesia were compelled to quit their homes and join in the trek to the West, the Russian and Polish authorities offered him a measure of protection. But the dividing line between East and West, already hardening, severed all contact with the outside world and every attempt to induce him to leave Silesia for Berlin proved in vain. He died on June 6th, 1946, in his eighty-fourth year. His body was taken to Berlin, and from there to the island of Hiddensee where, for more than half a century, he had spent the summer months. He lies buried in the small village churchyard of Kloster; his coffin encloses, according to his wish, a handful of Silesian earth and a copy of his epic poem *Der grosse Traum*.

Hauptmann's life and literary career are roughly contemporary with Bernard Shaw's. It is illuminating to compare these two men who, each in his country, came to be regarded as more than mere successful playwrights. Both were carried to fame in the early nineties by that literary movement which swept Europe under the name of realism, or naturalism; both were antagonistic to middle-class society, and set out to reveal the hypocrisies on which it was based. But there the parallel ends. Shaw was, and remained to the end, a rationalist and a moralist. His characters rarely live of their own accord, but are impersonations of ideas. Moreover, Shaw is in the first place a writer of comedy; even his few serious plays abound in wit and paradox. Hauptmann, on the other hand, is essentially a tragedian; even in his comedies, tragedy is always close at hand. His approach to human problems is emotional, and he is at his best when he creates intuitively and, as it were, unconsciously. He is never concerned with ideas, but always with human beings. What message he has to convey is not explicitly stated by his characters, but implicit in their actions and their sufferings. Moreover, he soon abandoned the realistic and social plane on which he won his first successes. His work grew into new dimensions. He delved into history, legend, and myth. His poetic strain which, as an undercurrent, had run through his most naturalistic works, broke forth and carried him to regions far removed from any temporal or local limitations.

Although Hauptmann, particularly in the latter part of his life, contributed to every *genre* of literature, he will always be known first and foremost as a dramatist. It was in drama that his greatest faculty, the creation of live characters, found its

12

fullest scope. 'Drama is undoubtedly the greatest form of literature; all thoughts are thought dramatically, all life is lived
dramatically.' Hauptmann sees drama in all human existence;
life, for him, is in its essence an unceasing strife—a strife that
rends the heart of man from the first moment of his conscious
existence. 'The earliest stage is man's mind', he noted, 'plays
were enacted in it long before the first theatre was opened'.
Hence genuine drama is for Hauptmann in the first place a
drama of the mind, of character, and not of action. 'The more
complex the plot, the less there is of character. The simpler the
plot, the richer the character . . . What you give to the plot you
take away from the character.'

This basic conception of drama partly explains why Hauptmann's principal characters are throughout passive. They do
not act; things happen to them. Their tragedy springs not so
much from an excess of action, or of passion, as from an in-
sufficiency, an incapacity to cope with the exigencies of life.
Their keynote is suffering. However, Hauptmann's intrinsic
philosophy is not one of fatalism. His central theme, shaped in
countless variations, is redemption through suffering. In the
end, when tragedy has taken its course, the victim, though felled
by the force of circumstance, emerges as the true conqueror.

It was always to the weak and suffering that Hauptmann felt
himself irresistibly drawn—to those who are trapped in the
snares of fate, and succumb. But fate is not outside and above
man: it is born in his heart, shaped by his character, and is for
that reason the more inescapable. In the early naturalistic plays,
the causes of man's suffering are partly in his social environment, that is, in material circumstance. As Hauptmann develops,
they shift more and more to man's innermost self; in other
words, to the timeless problems of human existence.

It is scarcely justifiable therefore to see in Hauptmann's
abandonment of the naturalistic form, and his growing inclina-
tion towards poetic drama, an inconsistency or even, as has
often been done, a yielding to changes of literary fashion. His
entire life-work, though encompassing a great diversity of
subject-matter and literary form, springs from a single basic
concept of man and of life.

The mainspring of Hauptmann's work has often been stated
to be *Mitleid*—compassion. But this compassion is devoid of
any sentimentality or condescension; it is rather a profound
sympathy with man's suffering wherever he encounters it, a
genuine understanding of all human frailties. Within the whole
range of his work, there is hardly a villain, only men misguided

13

by weakness, thwarted by blind instinct or corrupted by social environment. It is this all-pervading humanism which gives every subject Hauptmann touches an unmistakable, intensely personal stamp. There is no essential difference between the poor washerwoman and the emperor of the Aztecs, between the humble drayman and Charlemagne, between the girl who seeks death in the village pond and the daughter of Agamemnon. 'Before Art, as before the Law, all men are equal', he says in one of his plays. Each of his multitude of characters is alive with the ineffable warmth of its creator's heart.

This intensely human appeal made Hauptmann throughout his life one of the most cherished and venerated writers of his country. His person no less than his works inspired affection: the almost magical spell his appearance exercised could be felt on many occasions, when it turned a near-failure into undisputed triumph. Moreover, his works have the peculiar quality of growing independently, as though endowed with a life of their own; many of his plays which, at their first appearance, found little response, turned into successes when revived. Although so huge an *œuvre* as his contains many single works which are second-rate or not fully perfected, there is scarcely one which does not fall into place when viewed as a link in the author's development.

This development has often been compared to the natural growth of a tree—an image Hauptmann himself liked to employ in his discourses on literary themes. His roots were deeply sunk in the soil of his native Silesia, where his ancestors, weavers, peasants, and artisans, had lived for many centuries. This German province, wedged in between two Slavonic countries, lies somewhat outside the main stream of European culture; it is more open to the east than to the west and south from which it is separated by the long range of the Riesengebirge. Its Protestant inhabitants are given to introspection and mysticism, which have left their mark on many sons of the country from Jacob Böhme and Angelus Silesius to the romantic poet Eichendorff. It is from this country, and from this people, that Hauptmann drew his best powers, returning to them time and again. The cloud-capped mountains of the Riesengebirge, rich in ancient folklore, the open plains stretching north of them, and the provincial capital of Breslau form the background of a large number of his works. The range expanded to include the country-side around Berlin, with its lakes and fir-forests. From these scenes of his youth and early manhood he branched out in many directions. His acquaintance with Italy, where he spent the winter months, and especially the journey to Greece made in his forty-fifth year, brought him into contact with the Mediterranean world, which held him under its spell to the very end. Hauptmann, like so many of his countrymen, was throughout his life drawn by the lure of the South which he felt to be the natural complement to his own northern world. Through his whole life-work there runs the dualism of North and South, while his contacts with the West or East are comparatively slight. (His personal acquaintance with the Western countries was limited to a short visit to England in 1905, when he received a doctorate at Oxford University, and two brief journeys to America, one in 1894 and one in 1932.)

It has been claimed that his creative powers weakened whenever he moved away, in his writings, from his original sphere —the scenes and people of his native Silesia. However that may be, he returned in the end to die in his house, the 'Wiesenstein', which he had retained for nearly half a century, and which he liked to call 'the mystic protective shell of my soul'. And it is a strange coincidence that within a few days of his death Silesia ceased to be a German land.

In view of the size and variety of Hauptmann's work—forty-two completed plays, twenty narrative works, and a large quantity of epic and lyric poetry—it is not an easy task to convey an adequate picture of his stature in a language almost wholly devoid of any live associations with his writings. One possible method—to select a few works as significant examples—may be discarded, for such a selection would always be arbitrary and dictated by personal preference. While emphasizing the more important works, I shall try to present a more or less complete synopsis of his production, since one of its essential qualities is its very range and diversity. Such an attempt, in the limited space allowed, will necessarily be rather summary, as even an acquaintance with the subjects and contents of most of the works cannot be taken for granted.

I propose to elucidate this multiform work under several aspects—naturalism, romanticism, hellenism, mysticism. These classifications are not intended as watertight compartments into which Hauptmann's various works can be placed, but rather as basic trends which underlie his entire output, and emerge more or less clearly in the individual writings. At the same time, these trends follow one another, to a certain extent, in successive stages, thus presenting something like a coherent picture of Hauptmann's development from the naturalism of his beginning to the mysticism of his end.

15

I

Naturalism

The first performance of *Vor Sonnenaufgang* (Before Dawn), at a Sunday matinée of the Berlin *Freie Bühne*, in October 1889, opened a new chapter in the history of the German theatre. At one and the same time a new dramatist and a new form of drama emerged. The twenty-seven year old author was at once acclaimed as the leading German exponent of the literary movement which had sprung up, almost simultaneously, in many European countries, and which was marked by such names as Zola, Tolstoy, and Ibsen. Theodor Fontane, the veteran Berlin novelist, hailed him as 'the fulfiller of Ibsen', while Ibsen himself, who met the young author once or twice in Berlin, welcomed his first play as 'a bold and gallant feat'.

In fact, Hauptmann's approach to drama was very different from Ibsen's. He was never concerned with the reform of society or with the promulgation of moral precepts. His characters are at no time exponents of ideas, but all-round human beings who live and act in their own right. They stand both inside and outside society. The conflict between the irrational and incalculable in man on the one hand and society on the other is indeed a basic motive of many of his plays. Hauptmann's conception of man's existence in the world is thus wider and less time-bound than Ibsen's. With Ibsen, the mainspring of tragedy down to his last works is frustration—the realisation that life has been unlived or wrongly lived. With Hauptmann, it lies in the very nature of man. 'Ibsen' as Hauptmann himself defined the difference, 'mostly sees the tragic element merely in a wrecked life. Tragedy in a full life is the greater one.'

What induced Hauptmann to adopt realism, or naturalism, as his form of expression was not any theoretical reflexion or conscious act of will; it was rather an intuitive awareness of his true capacities. From the somewhat spurious romanticism of his early lyrics, he had turned to an exact observation of life and a realistic portrayal of character. In his autobiographical account of the first twenty-five years of his life, *Das Abenteuer meiner Jugend* (The Adventure of my Youth), he describes this decisive step in the following words:

> It seemed to me that all epigones, and we too, had lost the ground under our feet. The works of literature were strung horizontally, as it were, like pearls on a thread. They had no

vertical dimension . . . As in a flash, I became aware that I was deeply and broadly rooted in life, and that it was this very fact from which my writing could draw its nourishment. When I read Leo Tolstoy's *The Power of Darkness* I recognized the man who had begun in the soil where I, after slowly gaining mastership, meant to finish up in old age . . . What did I care for the babble about naturalism? Why, man is made of earth, and there is no work of literature, any more than there is a blossom or a fruit, but draws its strength from the earth!

He goes on to relate how this revelation opened up to him the whole wealth of childhood reminiscences, his parental home and its surroundings, the Silesian country-side with its inhabitants of peasants and weavers. From this rich store he drew the scenes and the characters for the greater number of his plays, enlarged by the impressions of the following years, the Breslau Art School and the country-side round Berlin. Side by side with this new approach went the decision to introduce dialect into literature—not as a comic adjunct but as a medium of drama equivalent to High German or to classical verse. 'I wanted to give dignity back to dialect.'

It was a fortunate coincidence that Hauptmann was met in his intentions by the literary tendencies of the epoch which, in reaction against the shallow romanticism preceding it, found its true expression in a ruthless realism. These literary tendencies had a strong political and revolutionary tinge, for they went hand in hand with socialism and a pungent criticism of contemporary bourgeois society. In his formative years in Zürich and Erkner, Hauptmann came into contact with some of the leading socialist writers and scientists; his first plays, down to *Die Weber*, marked him as a revolutionary and an opponent of the established order of imperial Germany. Yet Hauptmann's early leanings towards socialism were not the result of any rationally conceived theory; they were the natural expression of his sympathy with all human suffering.

For the naturalistic writers, 'nature' was identical with the ugly aspects of modern civilisation—with poverty, moral depravity and crime. It was the task of the artist to depict these aspects faithfully while dismissing the 'beautiful' as romantic falsification. 'Art', according to the naturalistic theory, 'has the tendency to revert to Life'. It simply reflects to the smallest detail a given segment of reality, a 'milieu'. All the traditional devices of classical drama, such as monologues, asides, in fact

17

any dramatic development and climax, are rejected as being 'unnatural'.

Within the whole range of Hauptmann's work, only the first play, *Vor Sonnenaufgang*, conforms fully to these principles. The hero, Loth, is a socialist doctrinaire and reformer who visits a family of Silesian peasants grown rich through the discovery of coal on their land. This sudden wealth has completely corrupted them; they are given to drunkenness, gambling, adultery, incest, in short, every conceivable vice. The only one untouched is the wealthy peasant's daughter, Helene. It is only natural that she should fall in love with the new-comer in whom she sees her saviour. Loth, whose eyes are gradually opened to the rottenness of her origin, fears that the inescapable laws of heredity would work on their children, and leaves the girl. Helene takes her own life. The hero, in his zest for truth at any price, seems to hail straight from a play of Ibsen's middle period. He is the only one of Hauptmann's characters whose actions are governed by abstract theories and principles. It is in Helene that for the first time a typical Hauptmann character takes shape—the girl who obeys her natural instincts and is crushed by the force of circumstance. She is the first of a long line of heroines who, despite all their individual differences have some fundamental traits in common. All Hauptmann's women are closer than men to the irrational forces of life, and follow unreflectingly their natural instincts. In the oppressive gloom of this first play, what struck deeper than the social challenge and the faithful observance of naturalistic theory was the entrancing love-scene in which the unmistakable Hauptmann tone sounded for the first time, simple as a folk-song and glowing with human warmth. When the author was challenged that in this instance he had transgressed the principles of naturalism he made the characteristic reply: 'Can I help it that nature is also beautiful?'

The influence of Ibsen is still evident in the two following plays, *Das Friedensfest* and *Einsame Menschen*. Both are stern domestic tragedies, centring around topical problems of heredity and marriage respectively; both adhere strictly to the classical unities of time and place. The action of *Das Friedensfest* (*The Coming of Peace*) unfolds in a single night—Christmas Eve. It is a drama of unrelieved gloom: two generations, parents and children, are locked in a life and death struggle in the course of which the father has a stroke. Once again a woman, through her selfless love and purity of heart, seeks to bring peace of mind to the younger of the two sons.

18

In his next play, *Einsame Menschen* (*Lonely Lives*), Hauptmann fully found himself. Its central theme, a man's vacillation
between two women, was to recur time and again in his work.
The motto introducing the play, 'I put this drama into the
hands of those who have lived it', points to the personal sources
from which it sprang. The central figure seems at first sight a
maturer version of Loth, though his actions do not spring from
any preconceived principles but from his individual, highly
strung and nervous character. Johannes Vockerat is a young
biologist, married to a girl intellectually inferior to him. He is
captivated by a young Russian girl student who shares his
interests, and whom he asks to stay at his house. Their relation-
ship, at first purely intellectual, gradually turns to love. In his
conflict, unable to find a solution, he finally drowns himself.
Although this play still conforms strictly to the naturalistic
rules there is running through it an impalpable poetic undercurrent springing from deeper emotional sources.

It is with his fourth play, *Die Weber* (*The Weavers*) that
Hauptmann wrote the masterpiece of his early period—the
work that carried his name far beyond the borders of Germany.
This play is the supreme achievement of naturalistic drama,
at the same time transcending all aesthetic theories by its
dramatic power and emotional impact. On the surface, it is a
revolutionary drama and has been accepted as such ever since its
first appearance in 1892, though it is devoid of any pronounced
political bias. Its revolutionary impact is inherent in its very
theme—the rising of the famished Silesian weavers in the 1840's.
Hauptmann was inspired by childhood reminiscences (his
grandfather had been a weaver) and by his compassion for the
poor and suffering. The play is without a central character—the
real hero is the mass of the weavers from which innumerable
single characters emerge and fade like waves in a surging sea.
The five acts follow one another without appreciable dramatic
development, a fact which has given rise to the criticism that
the drama is 'static', a mere portrayal of a state of things
(*Zustandsschilderung*). Yet the dramatic action is immanent
in the very theme—the gradual deepening of the weavers'
despair, the gathering impetus of their resistance, culminating
in the rousing 'Weavers' Song', their attack on the manufacturer's house and, finally, their short-lived victory over the
soldiers called in to quell the riot. Although ending on a note
of triumph, the play is pervaded throughout by a sense of
fatality: the rising, one feels, is doomed to failure. In the end, an
old weaver, the only one who never stirred from his loom but

set his hope on Heaven, is killed by a stray bullet. The whole drama moves with the force of ancient tragedy. Although the thoughts and speeches of the weavers revolve on material needs, and their driving force is sheer hunger, there is a deeper impulse in their inarticulate clamour. '*A jeder Mensch hat halt 'ne Sehnsucht*' (every man longs for something). With *Die Weber*, Hauptmann moved for the first time outside the middle class which had been the main field of naturalistic drama and of his own earlier plays. The lower-class world it depicts became the social sphere in which his most successful plays were set.

Die Weber has its great counterpart in *Florian Geyer*, written four years later, the drama of the German peasants' revolt of 1525. This play had a curious fate. At its first performance, in 1896, it proved a complete failure, but when it was revived in the early 'twenties, after Germany had suffered defeat, it had a rousing success, and has been regarded ever since as one of Hauptmann's crowning achievements. In *Florian Geyer*, the author applied the naturalistic technique, for the first and only time, to historical drama. It is a vast canvas of the period, crowded with a teeming mass of clearly portrayed characters, and reviving the language of the time and of the particular part of Germany, Franconia, in which the action is laid. Yet the drama moves with the compelling force of a ballad. As in *Die Weber*, the true hero of the play is the numberless mass of the peasants who rise against their oppressors, the German princes, and are brutally subdued. But here their inarticulate impulse is embodied in a leader, Florian Geyer, the 'Black Knight'. A renegade from his own class, he sides with the peasants, inspired by a deep sense of justice. '*Ein brennend Recht fliesst durch sein Herz*' (a burning right flows through his heart). Unlike Goethe's *Götz von Berlichingen,* the classical play on a kindred subject, *Florian Geyer* refrains from any vivid action; it merely shows the effect events have on the peasants who are interlocked in endless talks and arguments. Moreover, Hauptmann shows only the last stages of the rebellion, its decline and final defeat in a welter of blood. This gives the drama, almost from the start, a sense of utter hopelessness. In the end, Geyer seeks refuge in the castle of his brother-in-law, a knight who has fought against him. He is betrayed, cornered, and falls, shot in the back by an arrow.

In his blend of strength and gentleness, Florian Geyer is probably one of the finest characters Hauptmann has created. The whole drama, despite its realistic detail, is suffused with a poetic quality which marks it as one of the great works of dramatic literature.

Here is the end of the fourth act: Geyer arms himself for his last battle, helped by Marei, a girl who has followed him everywhere:

Geyer: I thank thee, Marei! Where do we spend the first night after death?
Marei: With St Gertrude.
Geyer: And where the second night after death?
Marei: With St Michael.
Geyer: So will I greet St Gertrude from thee the day after to-morrow, and three days hence St Michael. Do not be afraid. Sing!
[As an old peasant sings a battle song Geyer is overcome with emotion, and weeps.]
Geyer: Gentlemen, I am not ashamed. I did not weep for myself.—Tighten the straps, Marei, I must feel the iron . . . My helmet! Fasten my arm-greaves! I want to be buried in them . . . Now I am ready. Fare ye well, dear brothers, it would be a miracle were we to meet again.
A Priest: Brother Geyer, the great fire burns low, I think, for a long while. But it is written in the Scriptures: A bruised reed shall He not break, and smoking flax shall He not quench.
Geyer: Make merry, brothers! Why should we not make merry? St Agatha went to her martyr's death as to a dance. The holy maid Anastasia despised death. And we are men!

Hauptmann's early plays are not confined to tragedy. He made his first attempt at comedy with the play following *Die Weber—Kollege Crampton*. But it is with his next work, *Der Biberpelz* (The Beaver Coat), that he accomplished what is undoubtedly his best comedy and, for that matter, one of the two or three great comedies of German literature. This play, too, is drawn from immediate observation. In his autobiographical account, Hauptmann tells of the years he spent in the neighbourhood of Berlin:

In Erkner I took up my old life with walks and observations of all kinds. I got to know the little people, foresters, fishermen, bargees and railway-guards; I watched a washerwoman studiously and with as much love as if she had been a bearer of sceptre and crown.

21

From these impressions Hauptmann drew his comedy *Der Biberpelz*—above all its central figure, Mother Wolffen, the shrewd washerwoman, a petty thief and rogue, yet a perfect wife and mother, warm-hearted and lovable. Her antagonist is the narrow-minded, reactionary district-counsellor Wehrhahn, who confines his activities to hunting down 'dangerous elements' while neglecting his official duties. The period is the last years of Bismarck's rule, at the time of the anti-socialist laws. Prussian officialdom and militarism are epitomized in Wehrhahn. Yet political satire is not the main object of the comedy; it is first and foremost, like all Hauptmann's plays, a portrayal of character, drawn in minute detail and imbued with a warm-hearted humanity. The play ends, in the true naturalistic manner, without a clear-cut solution; the heroine gets away with her theft, shaking her head in wonderment at the praise Wehrhahn bestows on her: 'Well, I don't know . . .'

Eight years later Hauptmann produced a sequel, *Der rote Hahn* (Conflagration), generally considered a weaker replica of *Der Biberpelz*. Yet there are enough new elements in the play to give it an interest of its own. The time is advanced to the first part of the reign of Wilhelm II. The moral degeneration of society, coupled with growing wealth, has spread further: the play depicts, instead of one individual case, a multitude of villagers, with their upstarts and informers. Mother Wolffen is now engaged in a large-scale fraud: she sets fire to her house to secure her insurance money. Despite her unbroken vitality, a sense of tragedy is present from the outset; in the end she dies, thus dodging the net that is closing round her. She, too, is one of those restless souls who, in their clumsy and inarticulate way, reach out for something beyond their grasp. 'One just wants to get out of the mess in which we all struggle along', she says towards the close; and when she dies she 'throws up her hands as with joy, stammering: 'One longs . . . one longs for something . . .'

The critical delineation of German pre-war society, concentrating on a strictly limited milieu, culminates in the tragicomedy *Die Ratten* (The Rats) of 1911. This is the only one of Hauptmann's plays (apart from the incomplete *Herbert Engelmann*) which is set in Berlin: the scene is a large tenement in the East End of the city. This human rabbit-warren, with its sunless backyards and staircases, its squalor, its medley of noises, forms the constant background of the action, or actions, for there are in fact two or three plots running side by side. The main drama centres on Frau John, a simple mason's wife, whose only child has died at an early age and who in her frantic desire to find a substitute, adopts the illegitimate offspring of a house-maid. Nobody, not even her husband, suspects it is not her own child. She clings to it with the desperate instinct of an animal, she hides it when the real mother returns to reclaim it: then, to rid herself of the mother's persistent demands, she induces her own brother, who is utterly depraved, to kill the girl. When the police come to take the child from her, she feels herself cornered like a hunted animal and leaps to her death. The squalid loft in which part of this tragedy unfolds also serves as a store-room for a collection of disused theatrical costumes, where a retired actor gives drama classes. One of his pupils, Spitta (in some ways a self-portrait of the author as a young man) upholds the prin-ciples of naturalism—'Before Art, as before the Law, all men are equal'—against the obsolete views of the old actor who insists on the conventions of high tragedy, as represented by Schiller. The tragic irony of this argument lies in the fact that all along a genuine human drama unfolds under their very noses, without their being aware of it. When Frau John interrupts their dispute the old actor, to clinch his case, points to her with mocking triumph: 'Here comes your tragic muse, Spitta!' And turning to her: 'Thank God that your quiet, secluded, peaceful life makes you unsuited for a tragic heroine!'

With admirable skill, Hauptmann presents in this drama both the theory of naturalistic art and one of its finest examples. Compared with the human impact of the drama, the social im-plications, as suggested by the title, *Die Ratten*, are of secondary importance. The tenement house presents, to a certain extent, a cross-section of German society in the years before 1914. The old actor, a stout conservative and nationalist, rails against 'the rats' (such as young Spitta) who 'are undermining our glori-ous new and united German Empire, and are gnawing at the roots of the tree of idealism'. It has been claimed that Haupt-mann, in this play, has foreshadowed the imminent downfall of the existing social structure. Over and above this, however, it is a poignant drama of thwarted maternal instinct, depicted with deep psychological insight and compassion.

Hauptmann's dramatic art reaches perfection in those plays where the setting merely forms the frame for the human drama of a single central figure. In these instances, his skill in portray-ing living characters merges with the full momentum of tragedy in the classical sense. The outstanding examples are the Silesian dramas, *Fuhrmann Henschel* (1898) and *Rose Bernd* (1903). Both plays are drawn from immediate experience: *Fuhrmann*

Henschel (Drayman Henschel) has for its setting the author's home (in fact, most of the characters are portraits of people remembered from his childhood, including his own father), while *Rose Bernd* is set among the Silesian peasants. In both works, the social background plays only an incidental role, and the drama centres on universal human conflicts. The drayman Henschel, a giant in physical appearance but of a gentle and ponderous nature, is tempted, after the death of his first wife, to marry his house-keeper, a callous, scheming creature. Eventually he comes to realize that he has been trapped, and that she is deceiving him. When the child of his first marriage dies he feels himself to be guilty; tormented by remorse, and unable to extricate himself from his plight, he hangs himself. The way this simple tragedy unfolds, the gradual breaking-up of this strong and, at the same time, vulnerable character has the compelling force of classical drama. *Rose Bernd*, on the other hand, treats a favourite theme in German literature—the girl who kills her illegitimate child. It is, in essence, the Gretchen tragedy in a modern setting. Rose Bernd, a vigorous, hot-blooded country lass, is seduced by her employer and expects a child. Challenged by her father, who believes in her innocence, she gives false evidence in court. The only one who perceives the truth is her seducer's wife, a kind, motherly woman permanently condemned to an invalid-chair. The scene between the two women, the old and the young one, forms the climax of the play. Without a word of reproach, Frau Flamm holds out to Rose the blessings of motherhood: 'There's one single thing I've learned: what it is to be a mother here on earth and how a mother is blessed with sorrows.' And then, as the girl breaks down in a speechless confession: 'Be happy! One should look forward to one's child . . .' But Rose kills the baby as soon as it is born. Then, out of her mind with grief, she gives herself up and is led away by the village constable.

Both *Fuhrmann Henschel* and *Rose Bernd* are essentially dramas of passive suffering, and of the ultimate loneliness of the human heart. Both the drayman and the country lass feel that they are hopelessly ensnared by the blind power of fate. 'I can't help it', says Henschel, 'I've just stumbled into it'. And Rose, in her despair, cries out: 'If only one wasn't so alone! One is too alone here on earth!' In these plays, Hauptmann's dramatic genius attains full maturity. Both Henschel and Rose Bernd transcend the limits of their social class and period: in their dumb and primitive way, they touch on issues pertaining to all times and all forms of human existence.

A further series of Hauptmann's naturalistic plays can be

summarized as *Künstlerdramen*, artists' plays. In the artist, the conflict between the individual and society—one of the fundamental conflicts in Hauptmann's dramas—is most acute. All his artists are painters, modelled on former teachers and colleagues at the Breslau Art School. It is interesting to note that the basic theme, in each case, is incompetence, due to a moral flaw, or a lack of talent, or both. This defect is treated either tragically or comically, but the borderline is not defined —the comic always has a touch of tragedy. In *Kollege Crampton* (1892), Hauptmann's first attempt at comedy (inspired, as he owned, by a performance of Molière's *L'Avare*), he portrays one of his former art-masters who is sacked for his incompetence and addiction to drink. The plot as such is negligible; the play is essentially a penetrating psychological study of an eccentric character, half comic and half tragic, lovable despite his moral defects. Hauptmann treated the same theme some twenty years later, in a tragi-comedy, *Peter Brauer*. Here the artist, harassed by an insufferable wife and family, has sunk to such depths that he earns a meagre living by mass-producing royal portraits and colouring photographs. By a stroke of luck, he is commissioned to decorate a pavillion in a ducal park; but when, after some months, he is discovered scarcely to have started on his work, he is ignominiously dismissed. Yet even here Hauptmann contrives to present the character with sympathy and human understanding.

The theme recurs with the full force of tragedy in *Michael Kramer* (1900), one of his most personal and most intensely moving works. Here the action centres on two opposite types of artist, father and son. The father, Michael Kramer, is a noble, great-hearted character, deeply conscious of the sanctity of his vocation ('Art is Religion'); but he lacks the spark of genius, and he knows it. The son, Arnold, has this spark, but he is morally unstable, of a malicious and bitter nature, and suffers from his unattractive physical appearance. All efforts on the part of the father to rouse him from his inertia and imbue him with a sense of responsibility prove in vain. Arnold, who is hopelessly involved in a degrading love-affair, commits suicide. The last act, in which his body is laid out in his father's studio, transcends the limits of realistic drama: the very language falls into a rhythmical pattern as Michael Kramer pours out his heart to a friend in what is in fact one long soliloquy.

[Michael Kramer is absorbed in the contemplation of his dead son and of the lighted candles.]

25

I am of the opinion, Lachmann, that one should not be afraid in this world. Love, it is said, is as strong as death. But you may confidently reverse the saying: Death is as gentle as love, Lachmann. I tell you that death has been maligned. That is the greatest deceit in the world. Death is the mildest form of life: the masterpiece of Eternal Love ... You did the same to the Son of God! And do it to-day as you did it then! And to-day, as then, he will not die!—The bells are speaking, can you hear them? They are telling it to the people in the streets—the story of me and my son; saying that neither of us is lost! You can hear it clearly, word for word. To-day it has come to pass; to-day is the day. The bell is more than the church, Lachmann, the call to table more than the bread...

Thomas Mann, in his commemorative speech on Hauptmann, observes how here 'the poet, almost without thought-content, or with an utter vagueness of thought, only hovers on the language ... And yet', he continues, 'these half-articulate words are full of feeling, a fundamental feeling of Hauptmann's writing, the feeling for the incomprehensible in man's cosmic-metaphysical fate'. Here are Michael Kramer's concluding words:

Where shall we land, where are we drifting? Why do we sometimes cry out with joy into uncertainty? We tiny creatures, abandoned in the infinite? As though we knew where we are going ... It isn't for the splendours of the earth! it isn't for the parson's heaven! it isn't this and it isn't that. But what—what will it be in the end?

The last of Hauptmann's 'artists' plays' is *Gabriel Schillings Flucht* (Gabriel Schilling's Flight), written in 1906. Unlike his other realistic plays, this is set on a small island in the Baltic—evidently Hiddensee, where the author for over half a century used to spend the summer, and where he now lies buried. The swell of the sea, the open sky, the cry of the gulls form a constant background. The main theme resumes that of *Einsame Menschen*: the man torn between two women. Gabriel Schilling, a painter, has come to the island to escape from an unhappy marriage and the claims of an overbearing mistress. But he is followed first by his mistress, a Russian Jewess, to whose hysterical protestations he soon succumbs, and later by his wife. The two women fight passionately over the man whose moral resistance is weakened by a latent illness. Driven to

26

despair by his hopeless embroilment, he escapes from his sick-room and walks out into the sea—his second and final flight. The drama is headed by a motto taken from Plutarch: 'Some say they had met Eunosthus as he was hurrying to the sea to bathe because a woman had entered his sanctuary'. The artist's tragedy springs from his moral weakness, which leaves him defenceless against his erotic entanglements. His defect is thrown into sharper relief by the contraposition of another couple, a sound, healthy artist and his young mistress who try in vain to save Schilling and restore his balance of mind. Although realistic to the smallest detail, the play has a peculiar transparency which seems to reveal a sphere beyond the surface reality. One of the characters speaks of 'the clear sensation constantly present here that behind this visible world another world is hidden'. And the final stage-direction, describing the nocturnal procession of fishermen carrying the body of the drowned man, runs:

> Dark figures are seen, fishermen who carry a litter on which Schilling lies dead. Fisherwomen and children follow . . . The procession moves silently from behind the shed, past the galleon figure-head. There is something hushed and unreal about the whole scene.

This play was especially dear to Hauptmann, who withheld it from publication for several years. 'It is not a matter for the general public', he wrote in a preface, 'but for the pure receptivity and inwardness (*Innerlichkeit*) of a small circle. A single performance of a perfect kind in a very intimate theatre is my unfulfillable wish.' The wish came true when *Gabriel Schillings Flucht* was performed in the little eighteenth-century theatre at Lauchstädt in 1912; from there it made its way to the regular stage.

The year 1912—Hauptmann was then fifty—marked a turning-point in his creative development. The long succession of realistic plays, ranging over more than twenty years, came to an end. Latterly, they had alternated with plays of a very different type; but on the whole, the naturalistic form was still predominant. The plays starting with *Vor Sonnenaufgang* and ending with *Die Ratten* include the greater part of Hauptmann's best known and most performed dramatic works. In the second half of his life, his creative powers turned to totally different spheres. Only in three plays, written after the First World War, did he once more adopt the realistic form which

27

had been his original domain—*Herbert Engelmann* (which remained uncompleted), *Dorothea Angermann*, and *Vor Sonnenuntergang*. These plays are realistic in that their dialogue is in prose, and their characters are set in a clearly defined modern milieu. Yet they are in many ways far removed from the earlier naturalistic works. The social sphere in which the characters move is the upper middle class; and no attempt is made to reproduce dialect, or even colloquial speech: the language has, on the contrary, a rather literary and stilted quality. Nevertheless, the problems treated are unmistakably Hauptmann's. In all three plays, the drama springs from a conflict between the central figure and its social environment; in all three cases, it ends with voluntary death.

Herbert Engelmann (written in 1924 but published only posthumously in 1952, with a completed version by Carl Zuckmayer) is the only one of Hauptmann's plays set in the immediate post-war period. The hero is a young writer who cannot rid himself of his war experiences and return to a normal life. He is arrested for murder and, although acquitted for lack of proof, commits suicide. The futile struggle of an individual against a hard-hearted and callous world is, in essence, also the theme of the two other plays. *Dorothea Angermann* (1926) is the tragedy of a young girl who falls prey to a brute of a man, and for many long and wretched years suffers for this momentary lapse, until she is driven to suicide. The period is dated back to the 1890's, the time of Hauptmann's youth; the two middle acts are set in America, reflecting memories of his early visit to the States. The story has a certain affinity to *Rose Bernd*; but it lacks the simplicity of the earlier play. The conflict is sharpened by the antagonism of the girl's father, a narrow-minded prison chaplain, who forces her into marriage with her seducer. Dorothea is a highly complex character, vacillating between blind submission to her husband and love for a better man who is yet too weak to save her. Finally she returns home, physically and spiritually broken, to face her father for the last time. In this closing scene Hauptmann recaptures his old power of striking to the heart.

The most important of Hauptmann's late realistic plays is undoubtedly *Vor Sonnenuntergang* (Before Sunset, 1932). The title clearly alludes to his first play, *Vor Sonnenaufgang*. But while the latter heralded the dawn of a new age, the former refers to the end of a single individual, a man of seventy, who has outlived his time. Hauptmann had come full circle: the road he had travelled in those forty-three years separating the two works could not be better symbolized. At the beginning stands Loth, the social reformer and doctrinaire, burning with moral righteousness; at the end the aged Mathias Clausen, a late exponent of the humanist tradition, who sees his world fall to pieces around him. A wealthy Silesian manufacturer and, at the same time, a highly cultured man of letters, he has made Goethe his idol. The very theme of the play—an old man's passion for a young girl—echoes Goethe's life-story. It is a favourite theme of Hauptmann's: as old Wann with Pippa, as Charlemagne with his youthful hostage, so does Clausen experience physical and spiritual rebirth in his love for Inken, a girl of twenty, who returns his love. The drama develops when his children object to his marrying the girl; his fiercest opponent is his son-in-law, a ruthless businessman, in whom he sees the embodiment of the new materialist age: 'Now I must watch the entire spiritual achievement of my life turning to hideous nonsense in his inexorable hands.' The conflict reaches a climax when he is declared insane; death remains the only solution. To his only friend he speaks of the 'strangeness, futility and desolation' of life, his isolation in an estranged world. His last words, as he takes the poison, are: 'I thirst—I thirst for the end'.

Vor Sonnenuntergang, which has been called a 'modern *Lear*', is clearly the work of an old man who saw his own world crumble before the challenge of a new era. A few months after its first performance Hitler seized power in Germany. During the remaining fifteen years of his life, Hauptmann's mind turned to regions distant from the realities of the present-day world. Only once, in a dramatic scene in *Die Finsternisse* (*Darkness*, written in 1937 but not published till after his death) did he treat a topical subject in a more or less realistic form. This one-act play can be regarded as an epilogue to *Vor Sonnenuntergang*: it was inspired by the death of a Jewish friend who also served as a model for Mathias Clausen. Owing to the Nazi persecution, the family was compelled to bury the dead man clandestinely. The play shows the bereaved gathering at a midnight meal; the whole scene is weighed down by a sense of utter hopelessness and despair. 'I feel', says one of the assembled, 'as though we were together on a black ark, on black billows, in black air . . . The black ark floats though the ages. The floods on which it floats do not recede. We are the citizens of the Flood.' At one point, the dead man is seen sitting at the table with three Biblical figures, the prophet Elijah, Ahasuerus, and St John. Reality dissolves into a mystic realm—a realm in which Hauptmann's mind, at this stage of his development, was moving. Darkness closes in on the small group of people, gathered for the last time. In the closing passage one of them pronounces the fate of the Jews: 'The Lord of Sabaoth has placed us in an element above the ground which our feet may not touch. Thus we drift along, persecuted, tortured, killed, Ahasuerean and without peace, but immortal in all eternity!' to which a Christian friend replies: 'This is true of all of us'.

II

Romanticism

1893 was the *annus mirabilis* of Hauptmann's career: it saw the first performances of *Die Weber, Der Biberpelz*, and the 'dream poem' *Hanneles Himmelfahrt*. It came as a great surprise when the acclaimed champion of naturalism brought out this little poetic drama, full of supernatural incident and luxuriant verse. Yet it was only the obverse of Hauptmann's genius, hidden until then, which found expression in this work. Nor was it an entirely new departure: in his early lyrics (collected in a volume, *Das bunte Buch*, but then withdrawn from publication) the young poet had given full rein to his romantic leanings. The juvenile epic poem, *Promethidenlos*, the fruit of his early Mediterranean voyage, is steeped in romantic introspection. In *Hanneles Himmelfahrt* (The Assumption of Hannele) this trend was for the first time realized in drama.

Nevertheless, there is a close connexion between this work and the early naturalistic plays. A modern critic called it 'the second part of *Die Weber*'. The *Sehnsucht* which spurs the weavers to their hapless rebellion here fills the soul of the poor village girl who, in her last hours, amidst the squalor of the workhouse, experiences the bliss of paradise. Realism and romanticism are here perfectly integrated. Real characters change into dream figures; the Sister of Charity assumes the features of Hannele's dead mother; the village schoolteacher appears to her as the Saviour who leads her into paradise. The feverish visions of the dying girl are always related to reality: the author takes great care to introduce poetic language only where the realistic plane is abandoned, and to let her fantasies mirror the experiences of her short earthly life. And after the heavens have opened before her, and angels have borne her to eternal joy, the space narrows once more to the gloomy workhouse, and the doctor coldly confirms her death.

Hanneles Himmelfahrt is one of Hauptmann's masterpieces. The deep Christianity, rooted in the Protestant mysticism of his native Silesia, and the burning compassion for human suffering which permeate all his works, have rarely found more poignant expression. With these words the 'Stranger' raises the girl from her death-bed:

> Thus do I take thy lowliness from thee. I grant thine eyes everlasting light. Let them be filled with the light of countless suns. Let them be filled with everlasting day, from dawn till eve, and from eve till dawn. Receive all radiant things, blue sea, blue sky, and the green plains of eternity. I grant thine ear to hear all the rejoicing of all the millions of angels in the million heavens of God. Thus do I set free thy stammering tongue and lay upon it thy soul and my soul, and the soul of God Almighty. With these thy tears I cleanse thee from the dust and anguish of the world. I will raise thy feet high above the stars of God.

Hauptmann's romantic strain came into its own with his 'German fairy tale', *Die versunkene Glocke* (*The Sunken Bell*, 1896) which was to become his greatest popular success. The main theme echoes the painful crisis in his marriage that the poet was passing through at the time. The hero, Heinrich, vacillates between two women—his simple down-to-earth wife Magda, and Rautendelein, an elfin creature, who inspires him to new and daring creative work. The significance of the play, however, reaches far beyond the personal sphere. It is, fundamentally, an artist's drama, elaborating the spiritual struggle of the creative man in his pursuit of the ideal; but here the theme is realized on a symbolic plane, with the aid of allegorical and super-natural figures. Once again the setting is the Riesengebirge; most of the characters are elemental beings, some freely invented, some derived from local legend. Here, in bare outline, is the story: Heinrich, a bell-founder, has cast a bell which is to hang in a new-built chapel high in the mountains. On the way a mischievous wood-sprite tumbles it down a precipice into a mountain lake. Heinrich, gravely injured, is found by Rautendelein, an elf-like maid, who restores him to life. Inspired by her love, Heinrich sets about to build on the mountain-peak a 'temple of the sun' which will outshine all the churches of the plain. The parson comes to recall him to his duty; but Heinrich spurns his exhortations. Then, one night, the 'sunken bell' in the mountain lake begins to toll, and his two children

31

appear as in a dream to tell him that his wife has died of grief. Seized by remorse, Heinrich leaves Rautendelein and returns to the plain. In the last act, while the unfinished temple goes up in flames, he makes his way back to the mountains, a dying man, only to find that Rautendelein has joined the lubberly Nickelmann down in the well. As he dies in her arms, he hears his 'sun-bells' far above him in the air.

Die versunkene Glocke represents Hauptmann's most complete surrender to symbolism, or neo-romanticism. The drama is cast in a blank verse of mellifluous beauty. Various influences have worked upon the play: there is the clear imprint of Nietzsche in Heinrich's proclamation of a new religion of Joy and his rejection of Christianity; and Shakespeare's *Midsummer Night's Dream,* Goethe's *Faust,* Ibsen's *Brand* and *Peer Gynt* have left their traces. Yet all these elements are integrated in a work which has sprung straight from the poet's heart. The fundamental theme underlying it, the conflict between paganism and Christianity, was to run through many of his later writings. Here, paganism is not yet imbued with the spirit of Ancient Greece, but still clothed in the symbols of Germanic mythology: it is Baldur, Freya and Thor who are invoked by the elemental spirits. Already an attempt is made to reconcile the two opposing worlds: at the close of Heinrich's rapturous 'hymn to the sun', the climax of his confession of faith, the figures of Christ and Baldur merge into one:

> So aber treten alle wir ans Kreuz
> und, noch in Tränen, jubeln wir hinan,
> wo endlich, durch der Sonne Kraft erlöst,
> der tote Heiland seine Glieder regt
> und strahlend, lachend, ew'ger Jugend voll,
> ein Jüngling in den Maien niedersteigt.

> Then shall we all draw nearer to the Cross,
> And, still in tears, rejoice, until at last
> The dead Redeemer, by the Sun set free,
> His prisoned limbs shall stir from their deep sleep
> And radiant with the joy of endless youth
> Come down, Himself a Youth, into the May!
> (tr. C. H. Meltzer)

It is interesting to note that perhaps none of the major works of Hauptmann has faded so much as *Die versunkene Glocke*; its problems, and the way they are presented, bear the distinct mark of the period. He was more successful where he contrived

32

to fuse realism and romanticism, and to let the symbols grow from a minutely depicted reality, as he did in *Hanneles Himmel-fahrt*. This he achieved again, though to a very different purpose, in the comedy *Schluck und Jau* of 1900. It was the first of Hauptmann's works to be inspired by Shakespeare into whose orbit he was drawn more than once in his later development. *Schluck und Jau* takes its cue from the prologue to *The Taming of the Shrew*—the age-old motif of the poor man who, for a single day, is made to play the prince. Sly, in Hauptmann's play, is split into two characters, Schluck and Jau: the one gentle, warm-hearted, and lovable, the other a crude, boisterous drunkard. The opening follows Shakespeare's play faithfully: a party of noblemen, out hunting, come across the two tramps by the way-side, and resolve, for a jest, to cloth them in princely attire. Jau is put to sleep and persuaded, on awakening, that he is a prince who has recovered from a long illness, while Schluck is made to appear as his wife—a role he performs adroitly. The princely court at which this prank is enacted has a distinct flavour of *As You Like It*; the various characters—the wistful prince himself, his sententious companion Karl, the jester Malmstein, and Sidsellil, the prince's capricious mistress—they all have their counterparts in the Forest of Arden. The very language—the alternation of rough, idiomatic prose for the tramps, with rich blank verse for the nobility—follows the pattern set by Shakespeare. Nevertheless, the work is unmistakably Hauptmann's creation: Schluck and Jau are two genuine additions to his crowd of simple Silesian country-folk; the deeper significance of their adventure, the interrelation of 'reality' and 'dream', is repeatedly emphasized. Towards the close, when the two vagabonds have returned to their old way of life, Karl points the underlying moral of the story:

> Gib dich zufrieden, Mann! Du hast geträumt.
> Doch ich, wie ich hier stehe, auch der Fürst,
> auch seine Jäger, all sein Ingesinde,
> wir träumen, und für jeden kommt die Stunde,
> tags siebenmal und mehr, wo er sich sagt:
> nun wachst du auf—vorhin hast du geträumt!

> Be thou content, my man! Thou hast but dreamed.
> Yet I, even as thou seest me, and the prince
> And all his huntsmen and his serving-men—
> We dream! And to each one the moment comes,
> Seven times upon each day, in which he says:
> Thou wakest now and hitherto hast dreamed!

33

(tr. L. Lewisohn)

Probably the most perfect integration of the realistic and symbolic is *Und Pippa tanzt!* (And Pippa Dances! 1906), 'a legend of the glass-works'. This work reflects the many facets of Hauptmann's poetic genius, encompassing as it does realistic portrayal of simple life, romantic folklore, and deep-rooted mysticism. Seen in the context of Hauptmann's entire work, the play forms a link in a long line of creative efforts, extending over the greater part of his life, from an early prose fragment *Der Venezianer* to his last unfinished mystic novel *Der neue Christophorus*. According to ancient local legend, some Italian fortune hunters had found their way to the Silesian mountains, and were accredited with magical powers by the local inhabitants. Pippa (the name is evidently derived from Robert Browning's poem) is a dancing girl from Venice who is wandering through the country with her father, a glass-blower. The whole work is imbued with the glittering lure of Venice, the distant dream-city 'where water is transformed into glass'. Indeed the tinkling of glass and of icicles (the scene is set in mid-winter) echoes through the play like magical music. 'Listen how the glass on the mountain fir-trees is ringing! Do you hear? The long cones are tinkling. It is nearly day-break, but bitterly cold.' Every character is in some way connected with the century-old glass-works in the mountains. Pippa, herself fragile as Venetian glass, is something like a symbol of Beauty which the men around her try to grasp, each in his own way. The one who wins her is Michel Hellriegel, the dreamer and poet—a wandering apprentice who hails straight from the heart of German romanticism, from the world of Grimm and Eichendorff. The two meet in a country-inn crowded with glass-blowers and woodmen. When Pippa's father is knifed in a brawl, a huge and savage glass-blower, 'old Huhn', carries her off to his lonely hut. Michel finds his way there, and the pair escape together over the snow-covered mountains. In the second part, the realistic plane is abandoned, and the characters assume more and more a symbolic significance. The scene is laid high up in the mountains, in the observatory of Wann, 'a mythical character'. Through his magic powers, he draws the couple into his abode, unaware that Huhn also enters in pursuit. Between the three men there ensues a mute, bitter struggle for Pippa. In the end, despite Wann's warning, Pippa dances to the music of Michel's ocarina, and falls dead as Huhn crushes a glass goblet in his hand. He, too, sinks down dead. But death is not the end here: 'She is once again far from us on her journey', Wann comments sadly, 'and he, the old, restless, uncouth giant, is once again after her'. Michel goes blind, but in his blindness he imagines Pippa is with him, and sets out across the mountains for Italy, the land of his heart's desire. Wann remains behind, resigned to his life of philosophical contemplation.

No mere summary can do justice to the poetic charm of this work. At times, it is true, the deeper implications remain obscure; but there can be no doubt that Hauptmann created one of his finest and most imaginative works in *Und Pippa tanzt!* The language rises imperceptibly from the colloquial idiom of the beginning to the rich poetic diction of the end. The opposition of Wann and Huhn, the sage endowed with supernatural powers and the sub-human brute, recalls Prospero and Caliban. Like Prospero, Wann strives to rouse Huhn, by way of a painful ordeal, from his bestial state—an attempt which is thwarted by the intervention of higher powers. 'Once again', he reflects as he looks at the body of the savage monster, 'the invisible hand that reaches through walls and roofs has crossed my plans and taken its prey'. In the figure of Wann, Hauptmann foreshadowed, as it were, a later stage of his own development. Wann is the first exponent of that mystic realm to which the poet ultimately turned.

Hauptmann never again combined so successfully the realistic and romantic within a single play. Most of his dramas belong to either the one or the other. A substantial part of his work consists of plays purely poetic and romantic, dealing with subjects from medieval history and legend. The impulse actuating him in these plays is totally different from that which prompted him to write the historical drama *Florian Geyer*. In them he aims no longer at a broad realistic portrayal of a given period, but concentrates on a single central character who dominates the action, and who reflects, in poetic transmutation, the poet's own spiritual struggles. Most of these plays centre on erotic conflicts, on the obsession of a man by a bewitching girl who leads him to salvation or destruction. The first, and probably most outstanding, is *Der arme Heinrich* (Henry of Aue, 1902) which takes its subject from the medieval epic poem of Hartmann von der Aue. This work sprang from an acute personal experience—a serious illness from which the author recovered to what he liked to call 'the *rinascimento* of the fourth decade'. The story of the knight who, stricken with leprosy, is flung from the heights of worldly splendour to utter misery, and is saved by the self-sacrifice of a saintly maid, assumes in Hauptmann's hands a deep significance. The physical disease is merely the outward sign of his spiritual fall from Grace, and his salvation is brought

35

about not by an external miracle but by his inner transformation, the awakening of the power of love. When the girl, Ottegebe, lies under the physician's knife, prepared to sacrifice her life for the stricken man, Heinrich breaks down the door to save her—and by this very act finds himself restored. No attempt is made to interpret the events psychologically: the drama moves on an entirely poetic and symbolic level, and both the affliction and the salvation of the knight are accepted as being of divine origin. Ottegebe, in her simple devotion and purity, is one of the most intensely moving female characters Hauptmann has created; while Heinrich's despair, rising to a frenzy as he digs his own grave in the wilderness, burns with the ferocity of a Job or a Timon.

Two other plays based on medieval legend, *Kaiser Karls Geisel* (Charlemagne's Hostage, 1908) and *Griselda* (1909), are not of the same order artistically. The first treats an episode from the life of Charlemagne related in a sixteenth-century Italian chronicle. Hauptmann shows the aged Emperor in the full stature of his power and wisdom, shaken to the core by his chance encounter with a fascinating harlot. All his attempts to keep her near him are thwarted by her passionate and sensual nature; for her, he is merely an old man. Finally she is poisoned by his chancellor; Charlemagne, gazing at her body, regains the strength to take up his imperial task. Here Hauptmann gives us another of those female characters who hover between innocence of heart and abandonment to their instincts, and, by sheer sensual force, gain power over a man far superior to them.

Something of this contradiction appears again in *Griselda*. Hauptmann gives the famous story from Boccaccio a novel interpretation. The eccentric Count Ulrich falls in love with a robust peasant girl, Griselda, and makes her his wife, against the wish of his family. After their marriage, they both undergo a profound change: Griselda becomes the most tender and devoted wife, whereas the count turns into a neurotic, jealous of his own child. He has it taken from the mother and abandons her. Griselda returns to her parents' farm; a few months later, she enters the palace as a common servant, summoned to scrub the stairs for the christening party. Her husband recognizes her and takes her in his arms as she stumbles with the child she is made to carry. Perhaps the simple story is encumbered by a complex psychology not quite in keeping with the period; the co-existence of love and hatred between the sexes is seen through modern eyes. The essence of the play is contained in the last lines:

Ulrich: Who has put this curse on me that I must torment you with every conceivable malice of my heart—you, Griselda, whom I love with a sinful love?

Griselda: Do you think that I have never loved and tormented you at the same time?

Ulrich: No!—I've heard the call of your heart. I wish I had heard it sooner! Who am I that I should resist this impelling cry which makes us tremble, powerless, you as well as me, Griselda?—Tell me how I must atone?

Griselda: You must love me less, my beloved!

Shortly after *Griselda*, Hauptmann conceived the plan for another medieval comedy, *Ulrich von Lichtenstein*, set in the same region of the Southern Alps which was especially dear to him. The completion of this play, however, was long delayed: it was published and performed only in 1939. During the long process of maturing, the original conception seems to have lost much of its freshness and charm. As it is, the play presents a colourful picture of the late Middle Ages, its central figure being the Quixotic knight-errant and minstrel who, dressed up as Venus, set out from the Tyrol to Vienna on a 'love-crusade'. The plot, laid in Venice and in a South-Tyrolean castle, is negligible: during the revels of a midsummer night, the mad knight is tricked by the lady he worships, and unwittingly united to his own wife whom he has sorely neglected. The comedy, couched in short rhymed couplets, tries to evoke, not quite convincingly, the spirit of the age of minstrelsy. Another medieval play, *Die Tochter der Kathedrale* (The Daughter of the Cathedral), published in the same year, 1939, was a product of the old Hauptmann. Its theme was taken from a medieval French play, but was worked into an intricate fabric. This complex drama, set in the Pyrenees, tells the story of two pairs of twins, two brothers and two sisters, who are heirs to two hostile dukedoms. The younger of the girls, Frene, had been abandoned as an infant, and was found on the altar of a cathedral. In the course of many adventures, the two couples find each other in love and, finally, the two countries are reconciled. There is a flavour of the fairy-tale in this story, and with its strange incidents and wondrous revelations it recalls the mood of Shakespeare's late romances, of *Cymbeline* or *The Winter's Tale*. Some of the scenes are laid in the magical Forest of Brezilian, another Forest of Arden, in which the lovers meet and live in idyllic seclusion. Pater Johannes, a hermit and sage, actually cites Prospero, Ariel, and Puck as supernatural spirits who govern man's destiny. Neither the action nor even the characters seem to matter: man is a toy in the hands of God, 'the weaver of all weavers', who weaves his web to no other purpose than his own pleasure. 'Wir Tisserands', says Pater Johannes:

> Wir Tisserands, wir wissen's allesamt,
> dass wir sein auserwähltes Spielzeug sind,
> Er hat mit diesem Wissen uns begnadet . . .
> Der Goldschmied setzt die Spiele Gottes fort,
> der Mime, der Jongleur, der Schöpfer, den
> die Muse Gottes tragisch inspiriert
> oder auch komisch.

> We weavers know we are His chosen playthings,
> And with this knowledge He has favoured us . . .
> The goldsmith carries on the plays of God,
> The masker, juggler, the creator whom
> The tragic or the comic Muse inspires.

With this underlying philosophy, the drama transcends the romantic sphere of the earlier plays: at this stage, Hauptmann's mind was already immersed in the mysticism which coloured all his later works.

III

Hellenism

In 1907—he was then forty-five—Hauptmann went on a journey to Greece. This experience marked a turning-point in his literary development as momentous as the Italian journey in Goethe's. Ever since his early Mediterranean voyage, the South had held a fascination for him; but it had always been focused on Italy which, throughout his life-time, became something like his second home. While the works of his first ten years were confined exclusively to his northern homeland, the horizon widened after the turn of the century. The lure of the South made itself felt in *Der arme Heinrich*, rich in glowing descriptions of the Italian landscape, and still more in *Und Pippa tanzt!*, with its nostalgic longing for the magic of Venice. But in the next play, *Gabriel Schillings Flucht*, of 1906, the hero says: 'From my sixteenth year, I have been travelling, by way of a very vivid imagination, every spring and autumn to Greece.' A year later, this dream came true for the author.

The fruits of Hauptmann's contact with Greece ripened only some years later; but the immediate impact is registered in his travel book *Griechischer Frühling* (Greek Spring), which illuminates his personality as much as his individual approach to ancient Greece. What Hauptmann sought and found was not so much the art, not the monuments of classical perfection, but the unchanging Mediterranean scene, still haunted by the gods and myths of the ancients. Rather than the treasures of the cities, Hauptmann explored the Greek country-side. For him, the Greeks were 'a race of herdsmen and hunters'; it was on his long rides across the lonely hills and sun-drenched pastures that he felt the living presence of the ancient gods.

One thinks of Apollo, one thinks of Dionysos, but one does not think, in these surroundings, of their images in stone and metal. One sees the gods here and there, luminous, immaterial, visionary.

Hauptmann's approach to Greece was predominantly sensuous and mystical. Following in the wake of Burckhardt and Nietzsche rather than of Winkelmann and Goethe, he penetrated to the pre-classical, archaic age and sought the Orphic, Dionysian side of the Greeks rather than the balanced harmony of their classical period. He visualized their temples in glaring colours, and their theatres reeking with blood; he recognized 'in human sacrifice the bloody root of tragedy'. 'Tragedy', he noted under the overwhelming impression of the ruins of Delphi, 'tragedy means enmity, persecution, hatred and love as life's frenzy. Tragedy means fear, need, danger, pain, treachery, crime, villainy, murder, incest, slaughter.'

This newly gained insight into the nature of ancient tragedy, in such striking contrast to the tenets of naturalism, wrought a profound change in Hauptmann's own concept of drama. Only after the Greek journey did he designate some of his plays *Tragödie*—a term never used for his earlier plays. Evidently, Hauptmann's approach to Greek drama was far remote from Goethe's or Schiller's classical humanism; if anything, it was closer to Nietzsche's concepts.

In Corfu, feeling the first rapturous impact of the Mediterranean scenery, Hauptmann started on a drama of Telemachus, 'to immerse myself completely in the Homeric world', as he noted. From this developed *Der Bogen des Odysseus* (The Bow of Odysseus). This work, which he completed only in 1912, opened what may be called the second phase of Hauptmann's creative life. It condenses in a terse dramatic action the last twelve books of the *Odyssey*, relating the return of the hero to Ithaca and his vengeance on the suitors. Significantly, the whole action is laid in the farmstead of Eumaios, the faithful swineherd; even the slaughter of the suitors is transferred to this bucolic scene. The gods remain invisible; but they are ever-present in the prayers of the humans and in the elemental forces of nature. Land and sea are more than a mere background: they are active participants in the human drama. The story is weighed down by a sense of tragedy alien to the Homeric epic. Odysseus appears in rags, almost out of his mind with suffering. The scenes with his aged father, Laertes, who lives in the wilderness, a demented beggar, have something of the frenzy and terror of *Lear*. Penelope never appears, but she is always in the minds of the others—cool, callous, secretly relishing the attentions of her suitors. When he has wreaked his vengeance, Odysseus turns wearily to his son, with the closing lines of the play:

> Was wird die Mutter sagen, Telemach,
> dass ich ihr schönstes Spielzeug schon zerschlug?

> What will thy mother say, o Telemach,
> That I her favourite plaything broke so soon?

Der Bogen des Odysseus is, essentially, a drama of homecoming, extolling the mystical powers of the native soil. Perhaps the most significant moment occurs when Odysseus, gradually recognizing his home-land, stoops to pick up a handful of earth:

> Biete
> Mir Helena—ich bin ein Bettler, habe nichts
> Ausser diesen Lumpen!—biete mir
> Die heilige Troja, wie sie ging und stand:
> Ein Korn von diesem Staube wiegt sie auf!

> Behold, I am
> A beggar and have nothing in the world
> Save these poor rags! Offer me Helen,
> Give me the holy citadels of Troy:
> I'd weigh them not against this grain of earth!
> (tr. L. Lewisohn)

Embittered by the criticism the play received on its first performance, Hauptmann wrote: 'He who knows of no common link with nature, he who has nothing in him of the contact with either the soil or the sea, he who does not know the great physical and typical experiences of our earthly adventure . . . is incapable of realizing the meaning of the work.'

How fully the Greek world had gained a hold on Hauptmann's mind can be seen from the fact that he introduced classical verse and imagery even in the *Festspiel* (1913) which he was commissioned to write for the centenary of the German War of Liberation. He chose the form of a huge puppet-play to be enacted on a stage modelled on the Greek theatre. The sequence of scenes re-enacting the historical events is crowned by an allegorical figure, *Athene Germany*, who extols, in solemn trimeters, the works of peace and the all-pervading power of Eros. The radiant vision of ancient Greece is set against modern Europe, rent by fratricidal wars:

> Noch schaudernd von dem Bad traumschwerer Nacht,
> betret' ich nun den reinen Gipfel des Olymps,
> die klare Heimat sel'ger Götter. Hoch hinaus
> mich weitend in des lichten Aethers andres Bad.

> Still trembling from the bath of night's black dreams
> I enter now Olympus' pure, unsullied peaks,
> The radiant home of blessed gods, expanding far
> And high into the ether's bright and different bath.
>
> (tr. B. Q. Morgan)

These lines foreshadow the way Hauptmann's mind was to develop in the years to come. More and more the ageless beauty of the ancient world served him as an antidote to the terror and confusion of the present day.

It is in the non-dramatic works of his later life that Hauptmann's preoccupation with ancient Greece came into full play. In the first twenty-five years of his literary career, that is up to 1912 (apart from three early prose pieces), his narrative works were confined to the two large novels *Der Narr in Christo Emanuel Quint* and *Atlantis*. In the second part of his life, however, epic writings in prose and verse balance, and at times even outweigh, the dramatic works. In his short novel *Der Ketzer von Soana* (*The Heretic of Soana*), published in 1918, he achieved what is undoubtedly his finest prose work and, for that matter, one of the masterpieces of German narrative writing. The story, laid near Lake Lugano, tells of the young Roman Catholic priest of a small mountain village who falls passionately in love with a poor herdsman's daughter and, through this

41

experience, is transformed from a zealous servant of the Church into a pagan renegade. Like the bell-founder in *Die versunkene Glocke*, the priest Francesco turns his back on the Christian lowlands and gains the freedom of the mountains, where he finds fulfilment in a rapturous union with nature. His transformation seems to him a 'mystic awakening' from blindness and ignorance into the full light of day.

This was a gospel which had little in common with that which he had previously learned and taught. It derived by no means from the pages and letters of a book, but rather came welling up through grass, plants, and flowers out of the earth, or floating down with the light from the centre of the sun. All nature seemed to be animated and eloquent. Formerly dead and mute, she became active, confiding, frank, and communicative. Suddenly she seemed to be telling the young priest everything that she had hitherto concealed.

The whole story, told in a prose of classic perfection, is a single paean to the life-engendering forces of Nature and of Eros 'who is older and mightier than Zeus and all the other gods'. In the pastoral scenery of the Alpine world, in the primitive life of the mountain herdsmen, Hauptmann's vision of an ancient Arcadia finds fulfilment.

This vision materialized, on an even wider scale, in the Utopian novel *Die Insel der grossen Mutter* (*The Island of the Great Mother*). This work served him as a refuge in the dark years between 1916 and 1924. Here the spiritual rebirth into a new life, in intimate contact with nature, transforms not merely a single individual who becomes an outcast from human society, but a whole community. The plot of the story is fantastic in the extreme: some hundred women, saved from a luxury liner that has met with disaster in the South Seas, land on an uninhabited island abounding in tropical vegetation enough to sustain their lives for an indefinite period. Among them is a single boy of twelve. Completely cut off from the rest of the world, they shed all the conventions of Western civilisation and establish a purely matriarchal society. When, presently, one woman after another gives birth to a child, the children are declared to be of divine origin (although it is made clear by subtle implication that the causes are quite natural). 'La recherche de la paternité' is made an official taboo which becomes the centre-piece of a new religion. A touch of irony and light-hearted humour is never absent from this phantasmagoria.

The novel moves on a plane remote from any other Utopian work: its purpose is not social or political but purely poetic. Under the magic spell of their new-found paradise, the ship-wrecked women return to a natural existence from which they view their former lives with contempt. The sinking of the ship symbolizes, to their minds, the doom of the man-made western world:

> We have slipped back, like caught fish, through a mesh in the net of civilisation into the open sea. Or you might say: together with our *Kormoran*, another ship has been wrecked in our minds—the ship of civilisation.

Hauptmann's description of life on the island is full of classical allusions; scenes and symbols of Greek mythology are constantly evoked. The very name of Phaon—the boy whose presence is of such vital importance for the survival of the community—has mythical implications. But the classical images merge with Hindu and Buddhist concepts: the worship of 'Mukalinda' as the procreating god goes side by side with that of 'Bona Dea' as the supreme goddess.

The matriarchal community is, however, threatened by the very existence of its male offspring. To forestall this danger, the women relegate their sons to the other side of the island. There the boys develop a society on completely different lines, practising crafts and even building a fleet to establish contact with the outside world. All efforts on the part of the women to maintain their matriarchal rule are swept away by the revolt of the men who, in a wild orgy, break down the artificial barriers and reestablish the natural equilibrium. 'What has happened and still is happening', Phaon muses as he watches from a distance, 'is one of the ever recurring acts of Nature by which, from time to time, she shakes off every artificiality'.

The whole work, with its free play of fantasy, its subtle irony, its philosophical reflexion, is clearly the product of a mature mind that views the world with amused detachment. Yet the mood from which it sprang is one of deep pessimism and weariness of Western civilisation—a mood that colours most of Hauptmann's works conceived during and after the First World War. From the grim reality of the present-day world he escaped into the serene vision of his imaginary island, with its perfect setting for an ideal human existence.

Besides venturing into the field of narrative prose, Hauptmann showed a growing predilection for the epic poem. It is through

43

this medium, more than any other, that his classical trend was developed to the full. The very use of the hexameter (his favourite metre) points to the fascination classical models exercised on him. Hauptmann employed the epic form in the first place to retrace, with the nostalgia of old age, vital experiences of his youth. After his sixtieth year, he showed a distinct tendency to record his own mental growth—both in autobiographical accounts and in poetic transfiguration. *Anna* (1921), a pastoral idyll, clearly modelled on Goethe's *Hermann und Dorothea*, tells of an early, unhappy love-affair the poet experienced as a youth of eighteen. Luz, the romantic hero, is in every detail a self-portrait of Hauptmann, drawn with the indulgent irony of the sexagenarian. A shorter elegiac poem, *Mary*, rich in classical metaphor, evokes memories of the days of his first betrothal. A third epic poem, *Die blaue Blume* (The Blue Flower, 1924), cast in the more austere *ottava rima*, recalls in dream-like visions the poet's early days in Capri: autobiographical reminiscences mingle with descriptions of the island landscape. A rapturous ride on dolphins and the vision of a bacchantic procession show Hauptmann steeped in classical imagery. All three epic poems sprang from an urge to retrace the emotional experiences and formative influences of his adolescent years: they anticipated the two large autobiographical prose works of his old age, *Buch der Leidenschaft* (Book of Passion, 1930), the self-searching account of the prolonged crisis which led to the dissolution of his first marriage; and *Das Abenteuer meiner Jugend* (1937), the detailed chronicle of his childhood and youth.

Hauptmann's preoccupation with his own past and spiritual growth was more than a mere by-product of his creative work. It was the direct outcome of the profound change he underwent in the later stages of his life. His way, seen as a whole, led from the external to the internal world, from the objective portrayal of reality to subjective introspection. This way brought him, as it did so many Germans, into the spiritual orbit of Goethe, even to the point of conscious emulation. Several of his later writings were directly or indirectly inspired by Goethe. This is true even of two of the principal works of his ripe age, the epic poem *Till Eulenspiegel*, which he wrote in his sixties, and the tetralogy of the *Atrides*, the fruit of his last years. Both works are the pre-eminent and final expressions of Hauptmann's Hellenism.

Till Eulenspiegel is, both in range and depth of vision, perhaps the most ambitious of Hauptmann's works. In it he set out to create the epic of our age. Developing out of the chaos of the post-war era, it served him as a vessel into which he poured the sum of his knowledge, his life's experience, his comments on the contemporary world. The position it occupies in Hauptmann's work can be compared to that of Goethe's *Faust*, with which it is linked in more ways than one. The poem is sustained not by a single character, problem, or conflict, but aspires to embrace the whole of life. 'This whole life, leading from temptation to temptation, is nothing but a comedy of mankind'—these words from St Augustine stand on the title-page.

The hero is a German airman of the First World War who finds himself on the street after the Armistice. Under the name of the legendary rogue, he drives his waggon aimlessly through the misery and strife of post-war Germany, posing as a jester at village fairs. He contents himself with the role of a mere onlooker, but one with an infinite capacity for compassion. Though endowed with a supreme sense of humour, he quickly succumbs to gloom, indeed to despair, at the human suffering and folly he is forced to witness. The further he progresses the more is he possessed by dreams and fantasies: his way, leading from reality to inward vision, reflects the way of the author.

The first half of the poem remains on a predominantly realistic plane: Till has several love adventures; he witnesses the murder of a pacifist nobleman by a young fanatic, and the desperate remorse of the murderer; he watches the nationalist rising known as the *Kapp Putsch*, and the general strike of the workers which ended it; he stays as a guest of honour at the mock court of one of the German ex-kings, and later joins a group of gipsies camping in the woods. He is beset throughout by dreams and hallucinations; perhaps the most powerful is his story of what would happen on earth if, one day, the sun should fail to rise. In the second half of the work, these visions get the upper hand. His humour, bitter and caustic from the start, turns more and more to despair. He imagines himself appearing as the Emperor at a medieval council in Wittenberg, where exponents of various creeds, ranging from Hinduism to Communism, rail at one another. The whole scene ends in utter confusion, leaving Till weeping helplessly at the futility of all human endeavour:

> ... Ich beweine mein Volk! Ich beweine
> den unendlich mühseligen, dornigen Aufstieg der Menschheit!
> Ich beweine den ewigen Krieg, den kein Friede je abschliesst!
> Ich beweine den Glauben, beweine so Wissen als Irrtum!

Gott am Kreuze bewein' ich, den Statthalter Christi und seinen
Gegenpapst, Martin Luther, sie alle bewein' ich, bewein' ich!
Ich beweine auch die, die am Volke verblutet, verblutet
an der Menschheit, verblutet im Krieg und verblutet am Glauben!
die am Wissen verblutet und die da verblutet am Irrtum,
die verblutet für Christum am Kreuze, verblutet für seinen
mächt'gen Hirten zu Rom und die, die verblutet für Luther!

... I lament my people! I lament
the endless, strenuous, thorny ascent of mankind,
I lament perennial war which no peace will ever end,
I lament faith, lament both knowledge and error!
I lament the Lord on the Cross, the Vicar of Christ and
his antipope, Martin Luther—all these I lament!
I lament those, too, who bled for their people, bled
for mankind, bled in war, and bled for their faith,
who bled for knowledge and those who bled for error,
who bled for Christ on the Cross, bled for His
mighty shepherd in Rome, and those who bled for Luther!

After this 'most bitter, most grave, most oppressive, and also
most dangerous experience', Till turns his back on the present-
day world and sets out in search of Helen, the embodiment of
classical beauty. His imaginary flight to Greece, on the back of
a brazen donkey, takes the form of a story he tells to his poodle,
his only companion in the waggon. The sight of the Greek
landscape acts as a purification; landing on the banks of the
Eurotas, he is met by Apollo, in the guise of a young herdsman:

Reinigung ist dein Ziel. Und der Ort, wo du bist, ist der rechte,
dich zu läutern und rein dich zu waschen vom Blute des Python;
denn es hat dich der Kampf mit dem Drachen der Urnacht
                                                      besudelt!

Thy object is purification. And the place where thou art is the right one
To purge and cleanse thyself of the Python's blood;
For thy fight with the dragon of primeval night has soiled thee!

At this juncture, the parallel between Till's road and that of
Faust is most evident. But it is not Helen he finds. Instead, he
lives out a pastoral idyll lasting 'a thousand years' with Baubo, a
buxom demi-goddess who acts as jester to the Olympian gods.
But he also delves into the darker regions of the Greek world; on
the back of the centaur Chiron, he sets out on a fantastic ride
through the underworld where he witnesses the mythical union

of Leda and the swan, faces the petrifying heads of the Gorgons, and penetrates to the very origin of life. After this final adventure, Till finds himself back on earth. The concluding canto, a kind of epilogue, shows him wandering through Switzerland, in a mood of serene resignation. His last imaginary encounter is with Jesus, who appears to him as a simple shepherd. Then, at peace with the world, Till ends his own life in a mountain stream:

Es verstummte sein Lachen, und schweigend empfing ihn der
Abgrund.

His laughter died away, and silently the abyss received him.

It is open to question whether Hauptmann succeeded in what he aspired to do in this work—to present a cross-section of our age, seen by an infinitely receptive mind. The sprawling epic is certainly not of equal poetic perfection in all its parts; often the verse is marred by harsh colloquialisms, and the train of thought obscured by a profusion of symbols. Yet it attains in various passages to a visionary power unsurpassed in any of Hauptmann's other works.

During the thirteen years separating *Till Eulenspiegel* from his Greek tetralogy, Hauptmann's classical vein was somewhat obscured by other trends. Nevertheless his continued absorption in Greek antiquity is reflected in a number of longer poems written in the 'thirties, such as *Helios und Phaeton, Der Heros, Der Knabe Herakles*, and a poetic scene, *Die drei Palmyren*. The final expression of his Hellenism, however, was in dramatic form—the four plays of the *Atrides*. This, his last completed work, written during the Second World War, realizes fully the conception of Greek tragedy Hauptmann had formed more than thirty years before on his visit to Delphi. It is as remote from the classical humanism of Goethe as from the psychological approach to Greek themes of the modern French and American dramatists. While retaining the full power and grandeur of ancient tragedy, Hauptmann penetrates to the pre-classical, archaic age when men felt themselves to be helpless tools in the hands of all-powerful deities. The central idea pervading the whole cycle is the struggle between the powers of Light and Darkness, embodied in Apollo and Hecate. From the outset, the powers of Darkness hold sway over nature and man alike; only in the end is the balance restored, and man redeemed from the curse hanging over him. It is against this mythical background that the action runs its course, leading from murder to

47

murder, until the chain is finally broken by the self-sacrifice of Iphigenia. Inspired by Goethe's plan of an *Iphigenie in Delphi*, as set forth in the *Italian Journey*, Hauptmann first wrote the concluding piece; only then did he unfold the whole story, adding the first play, *Iphigenie in Aulis*, and linking them by two one-act plays, *Agamemnons Tod* and *Elektra*.

The opening scene of the first drama strikes the keynote of the entire work: demoniac powers have once more invaded the Grecian world and swept away the precarious margin separating it from barbarism. The Trojan War, with all its tragedy and crime, is wrought by these powers:

> Die Erde hat gebebt. Der Menschen Städte
> erzittern, fürchten ihren Untergang.
> Was für die Ewigkeit gemauert schien,
> zerbröckelt knisternd, knirscht und wankt im Grund.
> Die Sterne werfen sich aus ihren Bahnen,
> die Erde fiebert und der Mensch mit ihr.
> Die Götter kommen wiederum zu Ansehn,
> die man im Wohlergehen fast vergass:
> sie zeigen drohend sich allüberall . . .
> Es geht nicht mehr um Wohlsein, Königin,
> ein Weniger, ein Mehr davon, o nein:
> es geht um alles!—Sitte, schöner Schein,
> der hohe Adel köstlicher Gewöhnung
> ward losgebundener Dämonen Raub . . .

> The earth has trembled. The cities of men
> Shudder and dread their end.
> What seemed built for eternity
> Crumbles and cracks, tottering in its foundations.
> The stars are flung from their courses,
> Both earth and man are as in a fever.
> The gods, all but forgotten in times of comfort,
> Come to be respected once again,
> And show themselves menacingly everywhere . . .
> What is at stake is no longer well-being,
> A little more or less of it—nay,
> Everything is at stake! Manners, fine appearance,
> Noble dignity of graceful custom
> Have fallen prey to unleashed demons . . .

Undoubtedly the war during which the work was written left its imprint on this and similar passages. All the characters act as it were in a blind frenzy, unable to escape the vortex

48

into which they are irresistibly drawn. Agamemnon, struggling in vain to prevent the sacrifice of his daughter, succumbs eventually to the force of fate; Iphigenia offers herself, in a state of ecstasy, for the sacrifice. Without a will of her own, she falls under the spell of Hecate whose black ship is seen all along anchored in the bay. In the end, she is carried by this very ship to Tauris, to become a priestess to the pitiless deity.

The same sense of inexorable fate permeates *Agamemnons Tod* and *Elektra*. The scene of both plays is not the traditional one, in front of the palace of Mycene, but a lonely temple of Demeter, the earth-goddess; nor does Agamemnon, on his return from Troy, appear in regal splendour but as 'a huge beggar in rags' who has suffered shipwreck—very much like Odysseus in Hauptmann's earlier play. The action is reduced to its bare essentials, leading from the murder of Agamemnon to Orestes' retribution. The two plays are not really independent, but merely necessary links connecting the two Iphigenia dramas.

Iphigenie in Delphi, the last of the cycle, is somewhat different in character from the preceding plays. With its unity of time and place, sustained throughout three acts, and its background of the Delphic ritual, it has more of the statuesque grandeur of classical drama. Its dominant theme is redemption and reconciliation. In the first part, the powers of darkness still seem to rule supreme: both Electra and Orestes meet at the Delphic sanctuary, one seeking to render up the fateful axe, the other to find deliverance from the Furies. Orestes is followed by Iphigenia, whom he has brought from Tauris but whom he still fails to recognize. Once more the curse seems to take effect; Electra raises the axe against her sister, believing she has sacrificed Orestes. This scene is the turning-point; both Electra and Orestes, recognizing each other, regain their mental balance; Iphigenia, however, after revealing her identity, throws herself into a ravine and through her self-sacrifice raises the fatal curse hanging over her house.

Hauptmann's Iphigenia has little in common with Goethe's, the embodiment of 'pure humanity'. She feels herself irrevocably pledged to Hecate and has actually offered human sacrifices in her service. To her mind she did in fact suffer death when she was carried off from Aulis, and ever since has severed all links with the world of the living. Electra catches a glimpse of her true condition:

Elektra: Ein Seufzen ungestillter Sehnsucht ist,
    wo du auch gehst und stehst, um dich verbreitet.

> Du scheinst mir, Hohe, wie ein Schmerz, der wandelt –
> nein, mehr: als wie der Schmerz der ganzen Welt.

Iphigenie: Zu wenig und zu viel ist, was du sagst.
Von zugemessenen Schmerzen trägt die Welt
die kleinere Last, der Einzelne die grosse.
Doch willst du, Danaide, mich vergleichen,
nenne mich lieber: einen Tod, der wandelt.

Electra: A sigh of unstilled longing is about thee
wherever thou goest, noble one.
Thou seemest to me like a walking sorrow,
or rather, like the sorrow of the whole world.

Iphigenia: Too little and too much is what thou sayest.
Of the allotted sorrows, the world bears
the smaller burden, the single man the greater.
But if thou wilt liken me to something,
call me rather: a walking death.

By her self-destruction at the end of the drama Iphigenia merely realizes this knowledge.

This vast dramatic cycle, which Hauptmann completed at the age of eighty-two, reflects the profound pessimism of his final phase, deepened by the war during which it was written. The vision of ancient Greece no longer served him as an antidote to reality, as it did after the first war; it is itself suffused and transformed by this reality. Moreover, side by side with the stark realism of the foreground, there is throughout a sense of a second, invisible world, a realm of dark powers dominating the lives of men. Hauptmann's Hellenism, at this final stage, merges with the mysticism which sprang from deeper levels of his mind.

IV

Mysticism

In tracing Gerhart Hauptmann's development in three main streams, the naturalistic, the romantic, and the classical, an essential aspect of his work has been missed. It may be called his 'mysticism', though this term is rather more elusive than the others, since it applies not so much to a distinct form or subject-matter as to a quality which, to a greater or lesser degree, is inherent in all his works. It may be surprising, at a first glance,

50

to attach the name of mystic to a writer whose pre-eminent capacity was the presentation of reality; but it is apparent that even in Hauptmann's most naturalistic works there is an intangible undercurrent, something like a fourth dimension added to the surface reality. This undercurrent grew stronger as he matured, carrying him in later years to poetic realms almost diametrically opposed to his starting-point.

Hauptmann's mysticism had its mainspring in Silesian Protestantism which had found its fullest expression in such men as Jakob Böhme and Angelus Silesius. It was primarily Christian, although it was later to include Eastern and particularly Gnostic ideas. It was not of an abstract and speculative kind, but was one with his intuitive awareness of the elemental forces, the soil, the sun, and the sea. 'For Hauptmann', as one of his biographers puts it, 'the mystical is the inner side of reality'.

During the first phase, which was almost entirely devoted to naturalistic and romantic plays, concrete reality seems to predominate, although some works (for instance, *Hanneles Himmelfahrt, Die versunkene Glocke*, and *Und Pippa tanzt!*) move for long stretches on a supernatural and transcendental plane. The form Hauptmann's mysticism took in this phase was that of a simple Christian pietism, centring on the figure of Christ. In true Protestant spirit, he was concerned only with God-inspired man, that is, with the direct communication between man and the godhead, bypassing any intermediary and turning, often with bitter resentment, against orthodoxy in any form. The famished weavers, beyond their immediate material needs, are steeped in the spirit of the Gospels; and the rising of the peasants in *Florian Geyer* is first and foremost a religious movement. Hauptmann's Christian mysticism first manifested itself most forcibly in a non-dramatic work. In 1891, he wrote a short prose piece, *Der Apostel*, a psychological study of a vagabond who, in his religious transports, comes to identify himself with Christ. From this germ grew, almost twenty years later, the great novel *Der Narr in Christo Emanuel Quint (The Fool in Christ)*. It tells the story of a simple-minded religious fanatic who sets out from his native village to preach the Gospel of Christ to the poor Silesian country-folk. His message falls on fertile ground, fanning their innate mystic leanings into a religious ecstasy. By and by, as his belief grows more fervent, he identifies himself with Christ Himself. Various episodes and figures from the Scriptures find their parallels in the story: Emanuel Quint's foster-father is a carpenter; there is a Sermon

51

on the Mount, and a scene recalling the Last Supper; there is a group of devout disciples, humble artisans, who follow him blindly, among them an uncouth, savage fellow known as 'Red Joseph' who acts as Judas. But these casual analogies are not really relevant. The entire work is permeated with the Christian spirit of the particular brand alive in Silesia. Yet the narrative never dissolves into vague symbolism: the crowd of characters, weavers, artisans, smugglers, village schoolteachers and country parsons are seen with the sure eye of a realist. In the later parts of the book, as Quint makes his way to Breslau, the scene expands to include the townsmen, students, artists, and proletarians. At last, the path of the 'fool' is lost; we hear of his aimless wanderings across Germany, until he meets his end in the Swiss Alps—much as his worldly counterpart, Till Eulenspiegel, was to do in the later epic. In Quint's pocket a scrap of paper is found, bearing the cryptic words: 'The secret of the Kingdom?'

Hauptmann assumes throughout the role of a chronicler, relating the story with detachment. Yet it is evident that his heart goes out to the 'fool': 'how are we to know', he asks towards the end, 'whether it was not the true Saviour after all, who, in the guise of the poor fool, wished to find out how far the seed sown by God, the seed of the Kingdom, had ripened?'

Hauptmann's absorption in mystical problems explains his preoccupation with the religious upheaval of the sixteenth century. It gave birth to his drama *Florian Geyer*; it inspired a play *Magnus Garbe* (written in 1914-15 but published only in the Collected Works, 1942), a lurid drama of the Inquisition and a passionate indictment of religious fanaticism. For many years he also became absorbed in the story of the *Wiedertäufer* (Anabaptists) who had set out to turn the city of Münster in Westphalia into a New Zion. This subject Hauptmann tried to realize both in dramatic and in narrative form; neither was completed. But the extensive fragments reveal, in vivid pictures, the rise and fall of this sect and its leading figure, Jan of Leyden, who posed as a new Messiah. Later, elements of this work were used in a series of dramatic scenes, *Der Dom* (The Cathedral), on which Hauptmann was engaged in the years following the First World War. Here the scene shifts to a timeless plane, and the characters—Lucifer, Faust, Eckart, a Spanish Knight—attain the stature of symbolic figures. This work, too, remained a fragment. But its dominant vision of a Gothic cathedral, thronged with demoniac and satanic apparitions, recurs in several of the epic works, such as *Till Eulenspiegel, Die blaue Blume,* and finally in the mystic poem *Der grosse Traum.*

52

It is apparent that beyond the real world, as it unfolds in the greater part of Hauptmann's works, there is another sphere which is no less an essential part of his poetic universe. It extends, with many ramifications and cross-connexions, as a deeper, subconscious layer discernible in many of his writings, gaining in power as he grew older. It is reflected more frequently in narrative and poetic works than in drama which, by its very nature, demands more concrete and clearly defined presentation. Yet even the plays, especially the later ones, evince that 'magical' quality—the presence of a transcendental realm to which the actions and destinies of men are related. This realm is approached for the first time in *Und Pippa tanzt!*: Wann, who by magical power guides the lives of the others, anticipates those qualities which were to inform Hauptmann's later work. 'What would be the meaning of old age', he asks, 'if an old man were not more than a man?' But it was only when the author himself had entered the second half of his creative life that this magical sense began to be apparent in his writings. It can be felt in the only play published during the First World War, *Winterballade*, the dramatisation of a story by Selma Lagerlöf. In this tragedy of murder and retribution, set on an ice-bound fiord, the actions of men are governed by irrational powers. Hauptmann's growing tendency to escape from the reality of the present day into dream and fantasy is evident in the works conceived during and after the first war. This mood gave birth to *Till Eulenspiegel* and *Der grosse Traum*, to the Utopian novel *Die Insel der grossen Mutter*, and to the two poetic dramas *Der weisse Heiland* and *Indipohdi*, all of which were begun in the years 1912-1916.

These two plays, published simultaneously in 1920, are closely connected; both are set in the ancient Aztec civilisation, and both spring from the author's desire to escape to distant, exotic regions. *Der weisse Heiland* (The White Saviour), a 'dramatic fantasy', written in the trochaic metre of classical Spanish drama, pictures in nine scenes the conquest of Mexico by the Spaniards. The action centres on the tragic figure of the emperor Montezuma who, having welcomed the intruders as the divine saviours of his country, is then basely betrayed. A dreamer and visionary, solitary in his god-like status among men, he yearns for his own and the world's salvation. The tragic irony of the play lies in the fact that he is much closer to the essence of Christianity than his conquerors, and that the Spaniards eventually destroy in Montezuma's soul the very faith they have come ostensibly to kindle. He is rudely awakened from his delusion, and his trust

53

turns into bitter denunciation of the invaders. He is mortally wounded in an attempt to pacify his own people, and hurls his curse at the Spaniards:

> Raubgesindel! Fort! Vertilgt das
> Ungeziefer von der Erde!
> Legt Giftbrocken! Grabet Gruben!
> Stellet Fallen! Leget Schlingen!
> Ueberschleicht sie, wenn sie schlafen,
> mordet, mordet ohne Gnade
> dies Gezücht, das unsrer Mutter
> Erde Antlitz mit dem Unrat
> seiner Greuel so frech entehrt!

> Robbing fiends! Exterminate
> The unclean vermin from the earth!
> Poison their ways! Dig pits before them!
> Catch them in traps! Lay gins for them!
> Steal upon them when they're sleeping!
> Murder, murder without pity
> This white brood who desecrate
> The bosom of our mother earth
> With filth and abomination!

(tr. W. and E. Muir)

The shadows of disillusionment and weariness of living deepen in the dramatic poem *Indipohdi*. This too revolves round the legend of the 'White Saviour', but the issue is reversed: in *Der weisse Heiland* the genuine faith of the natives is contrasted with the barbarism of the Europeans; in *Indipohdi*, spiritual perfection is embodied in a white man who lives among savage natives. Hauptmann gives him the name of Prospero. The story is, in fact, a variation on Shakespeare's *Tempest*, but Hauptmann's island is inhabited by a native Aztec population, while the supernatural characters, such as Caliban and Ariel, are eliminated. The magic shifts, as it were, from the outer world into the mind of Prospero. The island with its creatures and conflicts, indeed the whole world of reality, appears to him merely as a product of his magical powers:

> Mein Leben ward Magie. Ich ward zum Magier.
> Es lag bei mir, Gestalten aufzurufen,
> gastlich sie zu bewirten oder sie
> mit einem Wink zu scheuchen in das Nichts.

Magic became my life: I a magician.
I had the power to call up shapes, to treat them
In friendly wise as guests, or with a gesture
To ban them back again to nothingness.

The drama develops as the magus strives to renounce this
world which still claims him. In Hauptmann's version, Prospero
has been driven from his dukedom by his son, Ormann. It is
the son who suffers shipwreck near the island and joins in a
revolt of the natives against the white man, unaware that he is
his father. Prospero subjects him to the supreme ordeal of
facing a sacrificial death. At the last moment he reveals his
identity and at the same time bequeathes his power to his son.
Then he ascends a mountain to end his life in a volcano—not
unlike Hölderlin's *Empedokles*. This last act, culminating in a
great soliloquy, contains the quintessence of the drama. Lit by
the rising sun, Prospero bids farewell to the world, lamenting
the ceaseless, murderous strife of creation:

> . . . Zerstückt des Haies Kiefer nicht
> des Menschen Leib? Ist nicht des Tigers Hunger
> qualvoller Hass und Mordsucht, und zerreisst
> er nicht Lebendiges und schlingt sein Fleisch?
> Ward eine Kreatur in diese Welt
> hineingeboren ohne Waffe, und
> die Mutter, die in Furcht und Grau'n gebiert,
> gebiert sie Furcht und Grauen nicht im Kinde?

> Is not the human body torn in pieces
> By the shark's jaw? Is not the tiger's hunger
> An agonizing hate and lust for blood?
> Rends he not living things and gulps their flesh?
> Was ever creature born into this world
> Without a weapon? And the mother
> Who bears her child in throes of fear and dread
> Does she not breed both fear and dread in the child?

But his last words are words of love and reconciliation:

> . . . Und es dringt
> wie leise Sphärenklänge auf mich ein
> vom Stern der Liebe. Nah ist die Versöhnung!
> Oh, reine Priesterin, nimm weg die Welt
> und schenke mir das Nichts, das mir gebührt!
> Ich fühle dich, ich sinke in dich! Nichts!

55

And from the star of love rays thrill me through
Like gentle music of the spheres. Redemption
Is nigh. O priestess, pure of heart, take thou
The world of sense away, bestow on me
That nothingness which is my fitting portion.
I feel thee, I am sinking in thee! Nothingness!

                                        (tr. W. and E. Muir)

The last stage-direction runs: 'Everything vanishes in mist'.

Undoubtedly while he was writing *Indipohdi* Hauptmann
intended it to be his valediction to life. In a conversation he
had shortly before his death with his friend and editor, C. F. W.
Behl, he described its import as 'the deepest and most painful
of all human tragedies, the way into solitude and nothingness'.

It might be said that Caliban, who found no place in Hauptmann's version of *The Tempest*, was given his own drama in
Veland, published five years later. Work on this went side by
side with *Indipohdi*; but its beginnings reach as far back as
1898. Its scene, too, is a mythical island 'full of noises'—but
now it is the storm-swept island of Nordic legend. If Prospero
represents man on the highest rung of spiritual evolution,
Veland, the legendary blacksmith, is man at his most bestial
level. Held captive by the king for the sake of his skilled crafts-
manship, he takes his savage vengeance by murdering the two
young princes and seducing the king's daughter. The play,
written in the trimeter of classical tragedy, is full of the gloom of
the heathen Norse world; the only glimmer of light comes from
a young shepherd who brings the Christian message of mercy
into the darkness of Veland's soul. Even in this soul there burns
a yearning for salvation; in the end he breaks his fetters and
soars into the air on his self-forged wings to challenge the gods.
Here, too, reality is engulfed in a magical atmosphere which
dominates every impulse and action.

After Prospero, the other Shakespearean character to stimu-
late Hauptmann's creative imagination was Hamlet. The Hamlet
theme occupied him for a full decade, between 1926 and 1936.
His first approach was an attempt to re-arrange and complement
what he considered to be a corrupt version of Shakespeare's
play. More important than this rather controversial experiment
were his own creative contributions to the subject, a novel
Im Wirbel der Berufung (1936) which revolves round a production of *Hamlet* at a small German court theatre, and an independent play, *Hamlet in Wittenberg* (1935) which forms a kind
of prelude to Shakespeare's drama. Most strikingly, the time is
advanced to the sixteenth century, thus bringing Hamlet into

contact with the Reformation. The young prince is caught in the spiritual upheaval that had its origin at the University of Wittenberg; a central scene shows him in a philosophical discourse with Melanchthon, the friend of Luther. Behind a mask of gaiety and juvenile exuberance, he is given to melancholia and gloom, despite his youth—he is nineteen—he feels old in this 'world of sorrow' which to him is a 'work of Satan'. He has a love-affair with a gipsy girl, Hamida, with whom he masquerades, at a students' festivity, as King Cophetua and the beggar-maid. But his prevailing mood is an unfathomable sadness:

> Die Trauer bin ich der verweinten Welt,
> der schwarze Mantel überm Himmelszelt.

> I am the sorrow of the weeping world,
> The inky cloak spread over heaven's vault.

All along he has a dark foreboding of the fate that lies in store for him; and the play ends with the arrival of messengers who announce his father's death and summon the prince back to Elsinore. *Incipit tragoedia . . .*

Despite its vivid dramatic action and its colourful scenes of medieval student life, the play is imbued with a sense of mystery emanating from its central character. It is the same quality that prevails in the plays of Hauptmann's last years, whether they deal with a romantic medieval subject, like *Die Tochter der Kathedrale*, or with an ancient myth, like the tetralogy of the *Atrides*.

During this final stage of his creative life, Hauptmann evinced a marked predilection for the short narrative, a form he developed in such works as *Die Spitzhacke*, *Das Meerwunder*, *Das Märchen*, and *Mignon*. Most of these novelettes hover on the borderline between reality and dream, evoking what he liked to call 'the third reality'. In *Die Spitzhacke* (The Pick-Axe) the poet imagines he is spending one last night in his father's inn before its demolition. In a bizarre flight of fancy, reminiscent of E. T. A. Hoffmann, he experiences a kind of Witches' Sabbath when heraldic beasts from famous inn-signs come to life to pay homage to the doomed house. The most striking of these tales, however, is undoubtedly *Das Meerwunder* (The Miracle of the Sea). The subject of this 'improbable story' is the passionate love of an old sea-captain for a woman who, after staying with him for a short time, is lost at sea. As it turns out, she was a kind of mermaid, a chimera who continues to haunt his imagination.

With a figure-head carved in her likeness he roams the seven seas and after being shipwrecked lives on a desolate South Sea island where he is obsessed by strange hallucinations. The mermaid, and the sea which is her element, symbolize the magic which surrounds reality: 'What we know of the whole of nature is as a small island to the ocean.' In the end, the captain is drawn into the element to which he was insolubly bound through his passion.

The last two writings of this type are the upshot of Hauptmann's preoccupation with Goethe: *Das Märchen* (*Fairy Tale*, 1941) refers explicitly to Goethe's similar little prose piece and moves in the same sphere of cryptic allegory and symbol. *Mignon* (which was published posthumously) brings to life not only the romantic creation of Goethe's fancy but the aged poet himself. The story, set in the serene landscape of the Lago Maggiore, relates the author's encounters with the Harper's daughter as with a live person, while Goethe himself appears in various disguises. The events are shrouded in an *aura magica* blurring the borderline between fact and imagination.

During the last years of his life, Hauptmann was at work on a long novel, *Der neue Christophorus*, which remained incomplete, and which can be considered the final outcome of his mysticism. The scene is set once more in the mountains of his immediate homeland. The roots of this work can be traced as far back as the 1890's; in fact, its themes and some of its characters accompanied him throughout the greater part of his life. They all centre in the figure of an old man endowed with magical power and superhuman insight. One of his first incarnations was Wann in *Und Pippa tanzt!*; at a later stage, he dominates a sequence of dramatic scenes, entitled *Galahad*. Around 1917, Hauptmann started on a novel, *Merlin*. Its first chapter describes how, one stormy night, a ghost-like girl appears in a mountain village and leads a party of men to a lonely grave in which they find a new-born child. This symbol of mystical rebirth forms the germ from which developed *Der neue Christophorus*. Its central characters are the *Bergpater*, a hermit living on the mountain crest, and *Erdmann* (Earth-man), the boy born in a grave, who becomes his disciple. The novel, on which Hauptmann worked until shortly before his death, is by its very nature interminable, a sequence of philosophical contemplations and discourses following the pattern of the novel of Goethe's old age, *Wilhelm Meisters Wanderjahre*. It served the author mainly as a storehouse for the sum of his ultimate wisdom and thought.

I have left the discussion of the epic poem *Der grosse Traum*

(The Great Dream) to the end, as it is perhaps the most significant creation of the mystic in Hauptmann and, next to *Till
Eulenspiegel*, the most comprehensive single work of his old
age. He began it during the First World War; he completed and
published it during the Second, in 1942. It thus accompanied
him for over a quarter of a century, during the last thirty years
of his life. In a preface he refers to the 'sombre introspection'
(*düstere Innerlichkeit*) of the war years from which the work had
sprung. The essence of the poem, he says, is 'twilight, inter-
penetration of day and night, of consciousness and unconscious-
ness. The aura of this bottomless world was a refuge for me time
and again during the war and the dire years following it.'

These words illuminate the nature of the poem and the prevailing mood in which it was written. Its inception belongs to
the same critical period of transformation and new departure
which also produced *Der weisse Heiland*, *Indipohdi*, and *Die
Insel der grossen Mutter*. Both in form and substance, *Der
grosse Traum* is modelled on Dante's *Divina Commedia*: it is
cast in strict *terza rima*, and it tells of the poet's imaginary
journey through the under and upper worlds, led by a spiritual
guide (at one time Dante himself). The affinity is explicitly emphasized:

> Mein Führer sprach: Du schreibst dein Epitaph.
> Von deiner Wanderschaft auf diesem Sterne
> nach hohem Vorbild willst du den Bericht
> hinüberretten in der Zeiten Ferne:
> Es machte der von gestern dir's zur Pflicht . . .

> My guide spoke: Thou art writing thy epitaph.
> Thou desirest to hand down to distant times
> the report of thy wanderings on this star,
> after the lofty model:
> He of yore made it thy duty.

But while Dante's journey leads through the fixed threefold
universe of the medieval Church, the modern poet has no such
pre-established world to draw upon; his way is a haphazard
flight of dark and light visions, without conscious direction.

Three levels of experience may be here distinguished—the
personal, the political, and the religious-mystical. The poem
opens in the personal sphere, with an invocation of the poet's
mother whom he sees as the embodiment of all motherhood,
exalted to the throne of God. It is to his mother that he returns

in the end, when his journey is done. His way leads him through the 'City of the Dead' where he encounters various former friends, and in particular his first wife, Mary, whose pale figure crosses his way time and again. The dream takes him further back, to the early days of his childhood; he sees himself standing, a boy of nine, beside his father, watching the triumphal entry of the troops returning from the Franco-Prussian War. At this point, the personal merges into the historical, the bright picture is obscured by a rain of gold, choking the very souls of men—a symbol of the material wealth showered on the newly established German Empire. The vision expands—the whole of Europe stretches at his feet, and the names of its great men, poets and musicians from Homer to Bach, ring in his ears. Again this happy vision is obliterated by the smoke and tumult of war. There is an apocalyptic vision of war's aftermath—ravenous beasts polluting the sacred ground of Europe and tearing to pieces vanquished Germany. Other passages may be interpreted as violent denunciations of National Socialism. The religious-mystical content, however, constitutes by far the greater part of the poem. It is here that the full range of Hauptmann's mysticism reveals itself, though it is often obscured by an excess of symbol and allegory. The poet dwells on the internal strife rending the Christian Church on the one hand, and the antagonism between Christianity and Greek paganism on the other. His denunciation of the Roman Church rises to a paroxysm of hatred. He visualizes a cathedral built over a crypt in which the Inquisition perpetrates its odious work; he sees an enormous spider, the Mantis Religiosa, devouring the very body of Christ. He has visions of Luther hurling the inkwell at Satan, of St Augustine pleading with God on Good and Evil. Throughout, Hauptmann is markedly influenced by Gnostic concepts. His spiritual guide, for most of the way, is Satanael who, according to Gnostic beliefs, is 'the elder son of God', combining within himself both Good and Evil, God and Satan. This deity appears as a beautiful youth, resembling a Greek god; at one point, he merges with the figure of Dionysos, leading a wild crowd of Bacchantes to the summit of Mount Parnassus where he is crucified by his own followers:

> Es hängt der Gott, eh man drei Punkte zählt,
> mit Nägeln angeheftet hoch am Pfahle,
> bespien, geschlagen, dornenkranzgequält!
> Essig und Galle barg nur mehr die Schale,
> nicht Wein mehr, die man seinen Lippen bot.

So hing er sterbend da, im letzten Strahle,
umflutet von Parnassos' Gipfelrot.

Before you could count three the God was hanging
high up on the pole, fastened by nails,
spat on, beaten, tormented by a crown of thorns.
The bowl offered to his lips contained
no longer wine but vinegar and gall.
Thus he was hanging, dying, lit by the last glow
on Parnassus' peak.

Once again, Hauptmann symbolizes in a striking image the
fusion of Christianity and Hellenism which was one of his fundamental concepts. Towards the close the poem re-echoes some
of the final passages of *Till Eulenspiegel*; in his quest of the
ultimate meaning of life the poet penetrates to the fiery centre
of the earth and, after this most terrible of all experiences,
finds himself in a serene Alpine landscape; once more, the
limpid beauty of nature acts as a purification after the night-
mares he has passed through.

With *Der grosse Traum*, Hauptmann reached the opposite
pole to his starting-point: the whole of reality is resolved in a
magic dream-world created in the poet's mind. Setting out as an
accurate recorder of realistic character he ended as a visionary.
Esoteric and subjective though this work is by its very nature,
it is no less relevant to a full comprehension of his creative mind
than any of his more celebrated works. How close it was to his
own heart can be understood from the fact that he wished a
copy of it to be buried with him.

Conclusion

I have tried, in the preceding chapters, to reduce the diversity
of Hauptmann's work to four main trends, partly running side
by side, and partly succeeding one another. Such a method
risks pressing the live writing rather arbitrarily into pre-con-
ceived categories. To grasp the unity of the mind that created
them all, we must step back and look at the work as a whole.

Any critical assessment of Hauptmann's work—at any rate,
of his dramatic work—will have to dispense with one of its most
vital aspects, its impact in the theatre. Indeed, the continued
life of his plays on the German stage for over half a century is
in itself a proof of their vitality. Among them, the earlier
realistic plays clearly stand highest in popular favour. Despite

61

Hauptmann's own partiality for his later work, despite the occasional revival of some of his late poetic dramas, it is the sequence of plays from *Die Weber* to *Die Ratten* that really lives to-day. What is the secret of their superiority? Hauptmann was unsurpassed in his own field, the delineation of realistic character. When he turned to poetic and symbolic drama, although he gained an incomparably greater range and depth of vision, he lost his greatest asset—the intuitive contact with the *Volk*, the simple people, where he had his roots. His verse, particularly in the later phases, often shows signs of carelessness, and is marred either by a cumbersome heaviness or by jarring colloquialisms. Hauptmann did not add a new voice to German poetry. Both in his lyric and epic poems he employed a rather undistinguished poetic diction; he seemed too hard pressed by the throng of characters and images to give sufficient attention to their embodiment in language. As for his prose, a similar defect can be seen in his later works. Many of them are marred by a certain awkwardness of diction, and tend towards the ponderous and sententious. Of all his prose writings, perhaps only two are quite devoid of these flaws—*Der Narr in Christo Emanuel Quint* and *Der Ketzer von Soana*, the two complementary novels written at the height of his power; here vision and language are in complete harmony.

The trend of Hauptmann's development has been compared to that of Goethe. Both were carried to fame by a literary revolution—with Goethe, the *Sturm und Drang*, with Hauptmann, naturalism—of which they at once became the representative leaders; both, by reaching out in new directions, soon transcended all doctrinal limitations; both reached a turning-point in their mid-forties through live contact with the classical heritage—Goethe in Italy, Hauptmann in Greece. Each experienced in middle-life a European war from which he emerged into a changed world, and each pursued in his old age his own independent course amidst the strivings of a new generation. Only their closing years were utterly different: while Goethe died in a peaceful era of hope and promise, Hauptmann, at the end of his life, looked into chaos.

The shadow of Goethe falls heavily across Hauptmann's mature life. He idolized the 'Olympian' to the point of conscious emulation; indeed Goethe's work directly inspired a remarkable number of his later writings. Yet, as creative types, Hauptmann and Goethe are opposites. Goethe's genius absorbed every form and every idea the world revealed to him; he was fundamentally undramatic; beyond the individual he was constantly seeking the universal law. Hauptmann was first and foremost a dramatist; his creative mind unfolded itself through characters, each with his own centre and his own law; he was concerned only with the individual. In the course of his development, however, Hauptmann came nearer to Goethe's approach; instead of abandoning himself to the throng of outer impressions, he turned more and more to creating from an inward vision. Whereas his earlier works reflected a given reality to the smallest detail, he later aimed at its symbolic interpretation.

This development from the specific to the general, the gradual withdrawal from the world of appearances to inward vision, constitutes a natural trend of almost every creative mind. With Hauptmann, however, it is accentuated by the fact that the faithful portrayal of reality was his salient gift and established his fame as a writer.

Of course, the life-like portrayal of character, the minute reflexion of reality, is not in itself a mark of great drama. Unless it contains that indefinable quality which raises the individual figure, or conflict, to something greater than itself, the best contrived play will remain a lifeless reproduction. What distinguishes a Hauptmann play is not the realism of the characters, nor is it the brilliance of dialogue or ingenuity of plot or situation. Still less is it an underlying 'idea' or 'problem'. In his entire work Hauptmann was never concerned with personifying ideas or problems: he was exclusively interested in human beings as such. Nor did he conceive his characters as representatives of any given form of society. This is the essential mark distinguishing his work from Ibsen's or Chekhov's. Both these dramatists move in a given social setting which determines their characters —with Ibsen, the middle-class society of his time, with Chekhov, the pre-revolutionary Russian gentry. There is no such common denominator in the works of Hauptmann. Whenever society, with its conventions and moral concepts, enters his plays, it does so as an inimical power, antagonizing and ultimately destroying the isolated human being.

As a matter of fact, most of Hauptmann's plays are not set within the middle-class but on its lower fringes, that is, among artisans and peasants—and among artists. These stand outside the accepted standards of a circumscribed society and are more closely linked to the elemental forces of human existence. The same applies to Hauptmann's women, who so often hold the centre of the drama.

The conflict between man's innermost being and outer reality, his inability to realize himself fully in a world determined by

63

social factors or by the callousness of others, is the essence of all Hauptmann's dramas. It is interesting to note how many of his central characters, both men and women, commit suicide. This has been wrongly ascribed to their inherent 'weakness'. It would be better to say that they are of a more subtle and complex nature, of a greater emotional capacity, than their fellowmen. Side by side with the actual artists, Crampton, Gabriel Schilling, Michael Kramer and his son, there are those possessed by an idea or immersed in a dream-world of their own; for instance the bell-founder Heinrich, Florian Geyer, Emanuel Quint, Michel Hellriegel and Till Eulenspiegel; or those weary of life, like Montezuma and Prospero. They all strive to realize their inward vision in the face of an adverse reality, and are broken in the attempt. Their guilt—if guilt it can be called—is not of a social or moral kind, but existential; it is inherent in their very existence as isolated human beings. Even the crowds of the weavers or peasants consist of so many individuals, each driven by his own inarticulate longing. '*A jeder Mensch hat halt 'ne Sehnsucht*'—these words of a simple weaver strike the keynote of all Hauptmann's characters; it is the longing for something ineffable, something beyond their reach, a fulfilment never to be granted in this life. Sometimes the presentiment of it finds expression in a final question—the question Emanuel Quint scribbles on a piece of paper before he perishes in the snow: 'The secret of the Kingdom?' Or the question Michael Kramer asks over his dead son's body: 'What—what will it be in the end?'

Hauptmann's dramas are tragedies of man's isolation. All his heroes suffer from one fundamental failing—an inability to communicate with others. 'Everything tends towards unity', Michael Kramer meditates, 'yet over us lies the curse of dispersion'. The evil characters, those who inflict suffering instead of enduring it, are beset by the same inability. There are, in fact, no villains in Hauptmann's world, only men thwarted in their natural growth. Even in the blackest soul there is an indefinite longing for the light, a divine spark. It lives in the uncouth glass-blower in *Pippa*, who utters inarticulate sounds about the *Finkla*, the 'little spark'; and Pippa, laying her hand on his chest, discovers with surprise that 'under his rags he is as white as a girl'. Or in *Die Ratten*, a man who has just committed a murder hears the church bells ringing; listening, he reveals his crime with the half-muttered words: '*Heute morchen halb viere hätt' se det Jlockenläuten noch heren jekonnt.*' (This morning at half past three she could still have heard the bells

64

ringing.) When Rose Bernd, the peasant girl who has been driven to kill her child, confesses the deed, she touches upon the keynote of her tragedy in a few simple words: *"s hat een' kee' Mensch ne genung lieb gehat'*. (Nobody has cared enough for me.)

Hauptmann's plays are full of such moments, revealing, in a sudden flash, the very core of a character. But they lose their significance when torn from their context. It is these momentary revelations, insignificant in themselves but striking to the heart, that make for the inimitable quality of Hauptmann's art. It is a quality which can only be defined as a profound humanism—an intuitive understanding of the timeless human drama.

Despite the prevalence of tragedy, the ultimate impact of Hauptmann's work is not one of pessimism. His negative attitude towards man as a social being is merely the reverse side of a positive belief in the healing powers of nature; all human existence is rooted in nature and longs to return to it. Throughout his work, nature is always palpably present. The narrative works are rich in glowing descriptions of its beauties, and in the plays its changing moods and manifestations form an essential component of the action. But nature is not merely the background of the human drama, it is the redeeming power and the ultimate refuge for man's suffering. Gabriel Schilling, before his collapse, raises his arms ecstatically towards the sea 'as if dazzled by a supernatural light in which he wants to dissolve', and cries out: 'The element! The element!' And when he has finally taken refuge in the sea, a friend says the concluding words: 'I think now he is safe for ever!' Again, in the story *Das Meerwunder*, the sea represents the purifying element into which the hero is finally drawn. Even more than the sea, the earth has a profound meaning for Hauptmann. In countless instances, he extols 'mother earth' as the source of all human striving. His favourite metaphors are the 'soil' and its associative images, 'humus', 'roots', and 'tree'. 'It is earth, mother earth, from which we are taken, and it is earth, mother earth, to which we must return.' The Odysseus drama is, above all, a panegyric in praise of the regenerating powers of the soil; through contact with his native land Odysseus regains his strength; and the dried-up springs of the island begin to flow as by a miracle. Young Hamlet, in his discourse with Melanchthon, praises the earth as the source of all life:

Steigt nicht der Baum, das Gras aus ihr ans Licht,
der Weizenhalm und jede holde Blume?

Und gingen wir nicht selbst zu guter Letzt
aus ihr hervor, der Erde? Sind wir selber
aus Wasser und aus Erde nicht gemacht?

Does not the tree, the grass rise from it to the light,
The blade of corn and every lovely flower?
And we ourselves—are we not sprung from earth,
Are we not made of water and of earth?

The young priest in *Der Ketzer von Soana* is moved to the depth
of his being when his eyes are opened to the powers of creation;
this revelation transforms him from a zealous ascetic to a man
living in rapturous union with the elemental forces. The same
is true of the shipwrecked women in *Die Insel der grossen
Mutter*, who find themselves thrown back upon a natural existence and develop energies hitherto unsuspected.

The most powerful manifestation of the elements, however, is
the sun. Something like a cult of the sun can be traced in Hauptmann's work. Heinrich, in *Die versunkene Glocke*, who sets
out to build his temple of the sun, calls himself 'the sun's
abandoned child that longs for home'. Even Emanuel Quint
combines his Christian fanaticism with an almost pagan worship
of the sun in which he sees 'the most powerful and profound
symbol'. Above all, the moment of sunrise assumes in many of
the works a mystic significance. Not only Quint but the central
figure of the novel of Hauptmann's old age, Pater Christophorus,
obeys a self-imposed rule—'always to worship the rising sun in
the open'. Laurence, the priestess among the women of *Île des
Dames*, makes daily contemplation of the rising sun the focus
of her mystic rites:

This birth of the sun represented the daily rebirth of man.
She saw in the rising sun the great awakening, recognizing a
mysterious connexion between sun and consciousness. We
live as much, and more, on the sun as on earth.

In a similar way, the glass-blower in *Und Pippa tanzt!* greets the
rising sun, 'his closed eyes turned to the East', with a wild cry of
triumph. And Prospero, as he ascends the mountain, opens his
final speech with an invocation to the sun, 'the mightiest minister of my magic hall'.

How deeply the worship of the sun was ingrained in the poet's
own heart can be judged from the fact that in his later years he
wrote a series of 'meditations' under the title *Sonnen* (Suns)—

philosophical reflexions he jotted down at the hour of sunrise. The first of them opens:

> The ageing poet stood in expectation of the sun. It rose behind a low bank of clouds. It resembled a rose-coloured mushroom—a tulip of fiery air—a water-lily—a turned-down ruby bowl . . . The ruby bowl breaks. Under its tremendous outburst of light the world is born.

This close communication with nature, at once sensuous and spiritual, forms the very basis of Hauptmann's poetic world. All his characters, even the most realistic, are rooted in it. Their various tragedies spring, in the last resort, from the clash between this elemental basis and the limitations of outer reality. Each one fails through his inability to realize his innermost self. This basic conception is the unifying principle, spanning the gulf between the realism of the beginning and the mysticism of the end; at first, the accurately observed reality is predominant, later, the inward vision of the soul.

Gerhart Hauptmann stands out as one of the last figures in European literature who aspired to encompass the full range of our Western heritage, combining in his work its two main streams, the Christian and the Greek. He himself was fully aware of his position in a changing world. Alluding to his last unfinished novel, *Der neue Christophorus*, whose hero is born in a grave, he said: 'My work is a beacon of the old time. But *Erdmann*, indeed, embodies eternal rebirth.'

APPENDIX

BIOGRAPHICAL DATES

15th November	1862	Born in Ober-Salzbrunn, Silesia
	1874-78	Attends Realschule in Breslau
	1878-79	Agricultural apprentice
	1880-82	Attends Art School in Breslau
	1882-83	Attends University in Jena
	1883-84	Mediterranean voyage and Rome
	1884-85	University in Berlin
	1885	Marries Marie Thienemann in Dresden
	1885-89	Lives in Erkner near Berlin
	1888	Studies in Zürich
	1889	First performance of *Vor Sonnenaufgang*
	1891-97	Lives mainly in Schreiberhau, Silesia
	1894	Visit to U.S.A.
	1901	Moves into his house 'Wiesenstein' in Agnetendorf, Silesia
	1904	Divorce, and marriage with Margarete Marschalk
	1905	Visit to England, Oxford D. Litt.
	1907	Journey to Greece
	1912	Nobel Prize, journey to Stockholm
	1932	Visit to U.S.A. for Goethe centenary
6th June	1946	Dies in Agnetendorf
28th July	1946	Buried on Hiddensee, Baltic

LIST OF PUBLISHED WORKS

Gerhart Hauptmann, Das Gesammelte Werk, 17 vols., Ausgabe letzter
Hand, Berlin, 1942.

Plays

1889 *Vor Sonnenaufgang*
1890 *Das Friedensfest*
1891 *Einsame Menschen*
1892 *Die Weber*
       Kollege Crampton
1893 *Der Biberpelz*
1893 *Hanneles Himmelfahrt*
1896 *Florian Geyer*
       Die versunkene Glocke
1898 *Fuhrmann Henschel*
1900 *Schluck und Jau*
       Michael Kramer
1901 *Der rote Hahn*
1902 *Der arme Heinrich*
1903 *Rose Bernd*
1905 *Elga* (written in 1896)
1906 *Und Pippa tanzt!*
1907 *Die Jungfern vom Bischofsberg*
1908 *Kaiser Karls Geisel*
1909 *Griselda*
1911 *Die Ratten*
1912 *Gabriel Schillings Flucht* (written in 1905-6)
1913 *Festspiel in deutschen Reimen*
1914 *Der Bogen des Odysseus*
1917 *Winterballade*
1920 *Der weisse Heiland*
       Indipohdi
1921 *Peter Brauer* (written in 1910)
1925 *Veland*
1926 *Dorothea Angermann*
1929 *Spuk (Die schwarze Maske—Hexenritt)*
1932 *Vor Sonnenuntergang*
1933 *Die goldene Harfe*
1935 *Hamlet in Wittenberg*
1939 *Ulrich von Lichtenstein*
1939 *Die Tochter der Kathedrale*
1941 *Iphigenie in Delphi*
1942 *Magnus Garbe* (in D.G.W., written in 1914-15)
1944 *Iphigenie in Aulis*
1947 *Die Finsternisse* (written in 1937)
1948 *Agamemnons Tod* and *Elektra*
1952 *Herbert Engelmann* (written in 1924)

Prose

1887 *Fasching*
1888 *Bahnwärter Thiel*
1891 *Der Apostel*
1908 *Griechischer Frühling*
1910 *Der Narr in Christo Emanuel Quint*
1912 *Atlantis*
1913 *Lohengrin (Gral-Phantasien)*
1914 *Parsival (Gral-Phantasien)*
1918 *Der Ketzer von Soana*
1922 *Phantom*
1924 *Die Insel der grossen Mutter*
1928 *Wanda*
1930 *Die Spitzhacke: Buch der Leidenschaft*
1931 *Die Hochzeit auf Buchenhorst*
1932 *Um Volk und Geist* (Speeches and addresses)
1934 *Das Meerwunder*
1936 *Im Wirbel der Berufung*
1937 *Das Abenteuer meiner Jugend*
1939 *Der Schuss im Park*
1941 *Das Märchen*
1943 *Der neue Christophorus* (Fragment)
1947 *Mignon*

Poetry, epic and lyric

1885 *Promethidenlos*
1888 *Das bunte Buch* [withdrawn and republished 1924]
1921 *Anna*
1924 *Die blaue Blume*
1927 *Till Eulenspiegel*
1939 *Ährenlese*
1942 *Der grosse Traum*
1946 *Neue Gedichte*

Translations

Gerhart Hauptmann, *The Dramatic Works*, 9 vols., Martin Secker, London, 1913-1929 and B. W. Huebsch, New York, 1912-1924

Hannele, A Dream Poem, translated by William Archer, W. Heinemann, London, 1894
translated by C. H. Meltzer, Dent, London 1950 (International Modern Plays, Everyman's) and Doubleday, Page & Co., New York 1908

Lonely Lives, translated by Mary Morison, W. Heinemann, London, 1898

The Weavers, translated by Mary Morison, W. Heinemann, London, 1899 and B. W. Huebsch, New York, 1911 and 1915

The Coming of Peace, translated by J. Achroch and C. E. Wheeler, London, and C. H. Sergel, Chicago, 1900
The Sunken Bell, translated by C. H. Meltzer, W. Heinemann, London, 1900 and Doubleday & McClure, New York, 1899
The Fool in Christ: Emanuel Quint, translated by T. Seltzer, Methuen, London, 1912 and Viking Press, New York, 1926
Atlantis, translated by A. and T. Seltzer, T. W. Laurie, London, and B. W. Huebsch, New York, 1912, 1913
Phantom, translated by R. Q. Morgan, M. Secker, London, and B. W. Huebsch, New York, 1923
The Heretic of Soana, M. Secker, London, 1923
The Island of the Great Mother, translated by W. and E. Muir, M. Secker, London, B. W. Huebsch and Viking Press, New York, 1925

Selected Bibliography

J. BAB, *Gerhart Hauptmann und seine besten Bühnenwerke*, Berlin, 1922

P. FECHTER, *Gerhart Hauptmann*, Dresden, 1922

P. SCHLENTHER, and A. ELOESSER, *Gerhart Hauptmann, Leben und Werke*, Berlin, 1922

M. PINKUS, and V. LUDWIG, *Gerhart Hauptmann, Werke von ihm und über ihn*, 1881-1931, Neustadt, 1932

F. A. VOIGT, *Antike und antikes Lebensgefühl im Werke Gerhart Hauptmanns*, Breslau, 1935
Hauptmann Studien, Breslau, 1936

C. F. W. BEHL, and F. A. VOIGT, *Gerhart Hauptmanns Leben, Chronik und Bild*, Berlin, 1942

F. A. VOIGT, and W. A. REICHART, *Hauptmann und Shakespeare*, Goslar, 1938

C. W. F. BEHL, *Wege zu Gerhart Hauptmann*, Goslar, 1948

C. F. W. BEHL, *Zwiesprache mit Gerhart Hauptmann*, Munich, 1948

W. ZIEGENFUSS, *Gerhart Hauptmann, Dichtung und Gesellschaftsidee der bürgerlichen Humanität*, Berlin, 1948

S. H. MULLER, *Gerhart Hauptmann and Goethe*, King's Crown Press, New York, 1949

J. GREGOR, *Gerhart Hauptmann, das Werk und unsere Zeit*, Vienna, 1951

TH. MANN, *Gerhart Hauptmann*, Gütersloh, 1953